A Memoir of a Portion of the Bolling Family in England and Virginia

You are holding a reproduction of an original work that is in the public domain in the United States of America, and possibly other countries. You may freely copy and distribute this work as no entity (individual or corporate) has a copyright on the body of the work. This book may contain prior copyright references, and library stamps (as most of these works were scanned from library copies). These have been scanned and retained as part of the historical artifact.

This book may have occasional imperfections such as missing or blurred pages, poor pictures, errant marks, etc. that were either part of the original artifact, or were introduced by the scanning process. We believe this work is culturally important, and despite the imperfections, have elected to bring it back into print as part of our continuing commitment to the preservation of printed works worldwide. We appreciate your understanding of the imperfections in the preservation process, and hope you enjoy this valuable book.

P_2V_2

WYNNE'S

HISTORICAL DOCUMENTS

FROM THE

OLD DOMINION.

No. IV.

" Gather up the fragments that remain "

No.----------

A MEMOIR

OF

A PORTION

OF

Bolling Family

IN

ENGLAND AND VIRGINIA

by Robert Bolling

PRINTED FOR PRIVATE DISTRIBUTION.

RICHMOND, VA.
W. H. WADE & CO.
1868.

EDITION OF 50 COPIES

INTRODUCTION.

The manuscript from which this memoir is now, for the first time printed, is one of the few historical waifs which, having survived the dangers peculiar to such frail materials, among a people too regardless of their value, and the hazards incident to the ravages of war, have been preserved, and, by a singular good fortune was returned to its original owner after a lapse of more than sixty years.

The memoir was written in the French language, by Robert Rolling, a gentleman of wealth, leisure and literary tastes, who has left other productions of his pen, of which, with some particulars of his history and accomplishments, an account will be found in the body of the work.

The original became the property of a member of the family, William Robertson, Esq. and in 1803 he gave it to his son, then a youth, as an exercise in translation. The translator has since then filled many positions of honor and trust, the evidences of the confidence his fellow-citizens entertained of his merits, and has for years been well-known as Judge John Robertson.

Subsequently the translation fell into the hands of John Randolph, of Roanoke, and was in his possession at the time of his death. It is well known, that he felt no little pride in his family history, and it is not, therefore, surprising, that he read the MS. with gratification, and showed his interest in it by inserting explanatory notes, by interlineation. All of these have been retained, and are to be found verbatim as they appear in the original, being added as foot notes and referred to by the letters in italics which occupy the places of the hyphens in the copy. He also wrote on the last page of the memoir the note, which will be found on page 12. This was subsequently crossed and recrossed with a pen, rendering it almost illegible. As the statements in it are correct, it is difficult to divine the object in defacing it. In March, 1868, this little volume was returned to Judge Robertson, with a note of which the following is a copy:

"The enclosed, found among Mr Randolph's papers, is sent to you by your old friend, William Leigh, who is too blind to write, or he would say something to you about former times, and the present evil days. He enjoys good health for one of his age (nearly eighty-five years old,) and would be glad to hear something from you"

"*Mecklenburg, January* 3, 1868"

To the courtesy of Judge R, I am indebted for the use of the MS and the privilege of printing a small number of copies, and by the kindness of gentlemen well informed in the history of our State, I am enabled to add, in the notes, much information which I am satisfied will be acceptable and instructive to all who are interested in such studies. Having been prohibited from using their names in connection with the work, I cannot express my obligations in a more definite manner.

To Mr. Thomas Bolling, of Bolling Hall, to Mr. Richard M. Bolling, now of Baltimore, and to Mr. H Q Holliday, of of Bolling's Island, I am indebted for the use of the family portraits and coat of arms, (now kept at the last named place,) and the privilege of having them photographed. It is a matter of deep regret, that no portrait of Mr Robert Bolling, the author of the Memoir, is in existence

It will be observed, that, though this memoir relates only to that branch of the family of the Bollings, which is descended from Pocahontas, yet its numerous ramifications include so many families, that it would have been impossible to notice them in a work of this size. I have, therefore, confined myself almost exclusively to the subject of the original memoir itself; giving but little more than the history of the family to the period named by the author, *i. e.* 1764. But, having accumulated a large amount of materials, while compiling what is embraced in this, it is my intention, to follow it up with a work on the descendants of Pocahontas, in which I will, so far as shall be possible, include all, of whom I can obtain any account.

Without farther notice, this fragment is commended to the favorable consideration of all who are interested in the history of our State.

T H W

Richmond, Va., July, 1869.

MEMOIRS

OF THE

BOLLING FAMILY,

WRITTEN BY

ROBERT BOLLING,

OF CHELLOWE, BUCKINGHAM COUNTY, VIRGINIA,

TRANSLATED

FROM THE

ORIGINAL FRENCH MANUSCRIPT

BY

John Robertson, Jr., son of Wm
1803

157,012

THE Bolling family is very ancient.¹ Robert Bolling, Esq., in the reign of Edward the IV, possessed the elegant house of Bolling Hall, near Bradford, in Yorkshire, where many generations of his ancestors had lived in the enjoyment of a private life. After his death, he was buried in the family vault in the church of Bradford, recommending his soul to the Most Holy Trinity, to the Holy Virgin, and to all the Saints. It is probable that his family had been benefactors of that church, and even had built it, since its coat of arms alone, was engraved upon it; which, perhaps, would not have been permitted, had it not been for that, or some other circumstance of the same kind. This Robert Bolling died in the year 1485, and was succeeded by many others of the name of Tristram, Nathaniel, &c., until, at last, Bolling Hall passed in succession to the family of the Tempests, &c.²

Robert Bolling, son of John and Mary Bolling (of the Bollings formerly of Bolling Hall), who lived in the parish of All-halloway, or Allhallows, Barkin parish, Tower street, London, the first of the name who settled in Virginia, was born in that large city 26th of December, 1646. He arrived here when only fourteen years of age, on 2 of October, 1660, and married, in the year 1675, Jane, daughter of Thomas Rolph,⁴ and grand-daughter of the Princess Pocahontas (wife of Mr. John Rolph), whose father was Powhatan, that Emperor of the Indians, who gave so much trouble to the English at their first establishment in his country.* He had by her only one son, John, born 27 January, 1676. After the death

*See the Hist. Virginia by Mr Wm. Stith. (Sic orig.)

of his wife, which happened in a short time, he married for the second time Anne, daughter of John Stith, by whom he had many children, whose posterity is still very numerous.⁶ This Robert Bolling lived at Kippax,⁶ in the county of Prince George, and dying on the 17 July, 1709, was buried there, aged 62 years.⁷ John Bolling, his eldest son, devoted himself to commerce.⁸ He had a gay, lively and penetrating spirit. He lived at Cobbs, on Appamattox river, where he received all the profits of an immense trade with his countrymen, and of one still greater with the Indians; and enjoyed at the same time all the pleasures of society, for which never was there a person better formed.⁹ It is probable that this Mr. Bolling had a very good opinion of himself. Being once in England to receive some inheritance, he found himself in the company of a lady from Yorkshire, (a place where language is much abused,) who hearing him speak, exclaimed in her country dialect, with much astonishment, "My God! only hear this gentleman, he speaks English as well as we do!" "Yes, indeed, madam," replied he, "and some hundreds of times better, or I should be very sorry for it."¹⁰ He married Mary, daughter of Richard Kennon of Conjuror's Neck, by whom he had one son, John Bolling, born 20 Jan'y, 1700, and five daughters:¹¹

Jane,ᵃ born in 1703; married —— to Richard Randolph} of Curls ¹²
Mary, in 1711; married to John Fleming.
Elizabeth, born in 1709; married —— to Dr. William Gay.
Martha, born in 1713, married —— to Mr. Thomas Eldridge
¹³ Anne, born in 1718; married —— to Mr. James Murray.

ᵃ My father's mother.

They have all been blesssd with that fruitfulness, formerly so desirable, which renders a family numerous, but poor " Mr. Bolling died at Cobbs, 20 April, 1729, and was buried there. His son, John Bolling, possessed the gay spirit of his father, without his taste for commerce From his infancy to the time of his death, he only studied his pleasure and amusement, which was, perhaps, pardonable in a man who was neither a gambler, a drunkard, nor a debauchee As he had no evil propensity, he thought himself entitled to enjoy innocent pleasures: Horses, Dogs, Hunting, Fishing, good Living, Dancing, his Wife and his Children, were the life and soul of Mr. John Bolling! He married first Elizabeth Lewis, daughter of John Lewis of Gloucester, privy counsellor of this colony, but this lady dying soon after without issue, he married (1st Aug. 1728) for the second time, Elizabeth, daughter of Dr. Archibald Blan, and niece of the famous commissary of that name. He had by her many children, some of whom died in their infancy: those who survived him are

Thomas Bolling, born 18 July, 1735.
John Bolling, born June, 1737.
Robert Bolling (the writer of these memoirs), born 28 August, 1738.
Mary, born 28 July, 1744.
Edward, born 9 Sept'r, 1746, and died 10th August, 1770.
Archibald, 2d son of that name, born 20th March, 1749.
Sarah, 2d daughter of that name, born 16th June, 1748
Anne, 2d daughter of that name, born 7th Feb'y, 1752.

Mr Bolling, to the end of his life continued to be fond of

good society. His house was open to every one, and the world, (I mean that small part of the world who knew him), were not ungrateful. The good will of the people gave him, for near thirty years, a seat in the General Assembly; and for a long time before his death he was at the head of the County Militia, as well as Judge of Chesterfield court.[15] He died at Cobbs, 6 Sept r, 1757, and was buried near his father and mother.

He divided his large estate among his sons, giving very little to his daughters.[16] To Thomas Bolling, he left[b] three-fourths of his Lickinghole plantation, and an island called Bolling's Island, in James River.[c][1-]

To John Bolling, the other part of Lickinghole; a plantation called Moulin, in Goochland; the tracts of Varina and Henrico, in the county of Henrico, with a small tract in Chesterfield.[d][1-] To Robert Bolling,[19] he left a plantation near Willis's Mountains,[e] another on James River, near the Seven Islands; and a small tract called Toleres, a league from the last in rising towards the source of the River. To Edward Bolling he gave the plantation of Falling River, that of Butcher's Run, on the River Roanoke, the house of Cobbs, a tract on Swift Creek, the Tobacco Warehouses in Pocahontas, a tract called the Old Town, in the county of Chesterfield, and also all the land he possessed in Amherst, which might probably amount to 6,000 acres.

To Archibald he left that part of his Buffalo Lick tract

---

b. Bolling Hall.

c. Containing 500 acres of land as rich as any on earth, now the property of Wm. B., son of the above Thomas.

d. Where he lived and died.

e. Chellowe.

which is in Bedford, together with Rack Island, (40,000 acres in all.)

To his widow he left, during her life only, some tracts already mentioned, viz. Cobbs, Old Town, Varina, Swift Creek and Bolling's Island, together with forty slaves. His other slaves, to the number of 150, were equally divided among his sons.²⁰

I have undertaken this little work because I have often regretted that my ancestors had never done it. Whatever regards them shall be always of importance to me, and the day perhaps will come when there may be persons desirous of knowing particularly what regards my brothers and myself. For that reason I will continue my relation, tho' I must speak of persons still living to the present day.²¹

1764.

Thomas Bolling was born at Varina²² on the 18 July, 1735, and lived with his father until his death (which happened in 1757,) except when he studied law, for sometime, under Mr. Robert Carter Nicholas, at Williamsburg.²³ He married his cousin, Betty Gay, daughter of Dr. Gay.

John Bolling possessed some of his father's dispositions; was like him, very large, and was six feet high. He delighted in the chase, and cared but little for the ladies, until he saw his lady. His character then as suddenly changed as that of Silvio in the Pastor Fido.²⁴ After many sighs, &c., he married Miss Jefferson, daughter*f* of that*g* Jefferson who, with Mr. Fry, made a map of Virginia.²⁵

Robert Bolling, (the writer of these memoirs, and I shall praise myself well,) was an accomplished youth, (I blush a

---

f. Sister of the late President S of the U.
g. Peter.

little, but take courage my friend, you are about to be a great man.) I say that Robert Bolling was a faultless young man. That nothing might be wanting to render his education complete, his father sent him to England—for good qualities even may be bought there. He departed from Hampton 24th of July, 1751, and arrived at London. 3rd September following. The vessel in which he sailed, was the Osgood (belonging to Mr. John Hanbury.) Captain Wilkie. Mr. Hanbury received our hero, as a man who esteemed his father. He did not, however, detain him long at London; he sent him in a hackney-coach to Wakefield, in Yorkshire, where he arrived (after having passed thro' Barnet, Biggleswade, Bugden, Newark, Grantham, Doncaster, Ferry-Bridge, &c.,) on the 24th of the same month.

Mr. Beverly, who was there with his family (viz: his wife, a son,[h] a daughter, a nephew of the name of Munford,[i] [26] and a son of President Fairfax, named William) went as far as Ferry-Bridge to meet him with a post-chaise, and carry him to his house. He lived then in West-gate street. On the next day, he was conducted to school, (the tutor being the celebrated Mr. John Clarke) and commenced the study of the Latin language. (I must now praise myself a little.) To tell the truth, he lost no time. As they perceived in him an astonishing genius, they did not cramp it at first by thrusting him into a class; and God knows how many classes he passed in the course of two years. He was then put in the same class in which were young Beverly, Fairfax and Munford, and about the same time began to learn French, of that language he was particularly fond, and soon acquired it under

---
h. The late Robert Beverley of Blandfield, Rappahannock river, Esq
i. The late Robert Munford of Richland, Mecklenburg, Roanoke river, Esq.

Monsieur DeBournai, (or as he was then called Monsieur des Bureaux) and afterwards under Monsieur des Granges, so that he understood it better than the Latin, notwithstanding the great progress he had made in that language. (Ah Mr. Bolling! my dear self, how many obligations do I owe you? I salute you with all my heart). During his stay at Wakefield, Mr. William Bolling, who lives at Ilkley, a village situated between Ottley and Skipton, became acquainted with him, and invited him to his house, during the vacations."

At this time, there lived with this gentleman, a lady of the name of Elizabeth Bolling, who possessed the tract of Chellowe, the rent of which might amount to 100 pounds sterling, a year.

She was a very agreeable girl, and altho twenty-five years of age, entertained as much affection for our adventurer, as if he had been her own son. Mr. Bolling will always remember the civilities he received from this family, with which he staid five weeks, on his first visit, and was there frequently afterwards. Miss Bolling married Mr William Prescott, of Halifax, where she resided when Mr. Bolling left Yorkshire, which he did in November, 1755 having quitted school the 11th of the same month. Mr. John Blair, (son of President Blair)" who studied law in Middle Temple, received him on his arrival at London, in his apartments, where he remained till the 14th of January, 1756, when he departed to embark at Gravesend, (the place where Pocahontas, his great, great, great grandmother had finished her days 1617)" on board the Swift. Captain Crookshanks, who was second captain of the Osgood

---

j. Afterwards Judge of the High Court of Chancery in Virginia, and subsequently, one of the Justices of the Supreme Court of the United States, appointed by Gen. Washington Associate Justice of the Supreme Court of the United States in 1789 in which office he died.

when she first passed to England. After a long voyage he arrived at York, on Good Friday, in the month of April. As the assembly was then sitting, Mr. John Bolling his father, who represented the County of Chesterfield, received him at Williamsburg. For want of paper I am obliged to abridge this history, suffice it to say, that Mr Bolling afterwards studied law (in the house where G Davenport lives,) under the direction of Mr. Waller.[30] There he was smitten by the charms of Miss Susanna Chiswell; she also was fond of him After this affair was concluded by a contract between that lady and Mr. Lewis Martin, he attached himself to Miss Miller whom he was desperately in love with, and who was equally smitten Mr Miller having lost his lady in 1757, conceived the resolution of returning to Scotland, his native country, and of carrying his daughter and other children, with him. He executed this barbarous design, and left Virginia the 16th of October, 1760, carrying with him that poor girl more dead than alive, and dying at London in the month of February, 1762 left her deserted and forlorn. Mr. Bolling wrote her, assuring her that his former sentiments for her, still continued. That letter was taken at sea. Having heard soon after that she had married Mr Blande.[11] Mr Bolling endeavored to forget her, and attached himself to Miss Mary (daughter of Mr William) Burton, of Northampton, E. S.* of Virginia, and married her at the Old Plantation in that county, the 5th of June, 1763. This amiable lady died at Jordan's the 2nd of May, 1764, two days after the birth of her daughter— Mary Burton Bolling.[12]

Mr John Rolph married Pocahontas, in the beginning of the month of August, 1613 [13] She was at that time 18 years

*Eastern Shore, comprising the counties of Accomac and Northampton.—ED.

of age, being born in 1595, she died at Gravesend in the month of February or March, 1617." Her husband was afterwards in the Council of Virginia formed in consequence of a commission from the Company.³⁵

Mary Bolling, wife of Robert Bolling. is buried at Cobbs. near Mr. John Bolling, the elder

The following note on the outside page of the last leaf of the manuscript is also in the handwriting of John Randolph, of Roanoke

"Robert Bolling, Esq., of Chellowe, in the County of Buckingham, in Virginia.* He was born at Varina in Henrico County, Virginia, in 1738, and died in the flower of his age some time before the revolution. He courted the muses, and left behind him two volumes of poetry in the Horatian style These volumes are said to be at Chellowe, were in the possession of his widow at Chellowe, during the Revolutionary War." He wrote equally well in Latin, French and Italian. Of these an Italian piece written by him, on himself; has been published in the second volume of the "Columbian Magazine," left in the possession of his executor, Colonel Theoderick Bland of Cawsons."*

NOTES

TO

THE BOLLING MEMOIRS.

NOTES.

(1) The origin of the races which made up the population of the Colony of Virginia, has excited a lively interest in our own times, and this interest is likely rather to increase than diminish, by the developments that are making every day in relation to the past. Hence the genealogy of any family in the Colony of Virginia has not only its own worth, but a distinctive value in association with those of other families. To trace a family to England has been regarded heretofore, as settling our inquiries upon the subject, but the question now arises, to which of the great branches of the English race does the family belong? to the Anglo-Saxon or the Norman? In answering this question we must mainly depend upon the names of the parties, and although this test is very far from being conclusive, as the Norman lieutenants frequently took their names from the Saxon estates which they seized upon, yet in the main it is the most available which we can adopt. And the question arises, to which of the two great branches of the English race do the Bollings belong? Evidently from the derivation of the name, which signifies "the sons of the Round Hill," (from *Boll*, a round Hill, and *ing*, the plural of the Saxon for *son*,) it is of Saxon origin. The name of Boleyn and Bullen belongs to the Normans; but Bouldin, a Virginia name, is a corruption of Baldwin, at a time when the spelling of words was determinable by the consonants mainly, and when a different vowel would be used in writing the same word in the same sentence. The word Baldwin, or its corrupt form, Bouldin, signifies the Bald conqueror, or the victory of the Bald man; and it would be amusing to inquire how far the heads of the present Bouldins are covered with hair.

(2) "Bowling Hall is situated at the distance of one mile from Bradford, and nine from Halifax, in the midst of fine scenery, at the head of an extensive and fertile valley, bounded by luxuriant hills, waving over each other, and overtopped to the north by the barren Heights of Rumble's Moor, at the foot of which glides the river Aire, which has its source in the small Lake of Malham-water, in Craven. The house, a large majestic building, with a centre and two deep wings to the north, has been built at very different periods. The south front, opening to extensive gardens, is terminated by two square towers of considerable but uncertain antiquity. The west tower, decidedly the most ancient, the walls of which are five feet thick, has been, it is conjectured, originally the entrance to an inner court, no traces of which now remain. The rest of the building may be safely assigned to the age of Elizabeth, or probably to that of her immediate successor, [in one of the lodging rooms in this part of the house, is the date 1615, over the fire place] and was doubtless erected by one of the Tempest family, who held the estate at least a century and a half.

"Bolling, as it was originally spelled, was the manor and residence of a family bearing the same name, from the origin of local surnames to the reign of Henry VII, when Rosamond, daughter and heiress of Tristram Bolling, married Sir Richard Tempest, of Bracewell, Kn't, and thereby took into that family, not only Bowling, but the manors of Thornton and Denholme, with lands in Clayton and Oxenhope. In this line it continued till the civil wars of the seventeenth century, when Richard Tempest, a weak, imprudent man, ruined partly by his own extravagances, and partly by his attachment to the royal cause, sold the estate to Henry Savile, Esq. of Thornhill Green, near Wakefield, the immediate ancestor of the present family. In 1668 Mr. Savile disposed of it to Francis Lindley, Esq., of Gray's Inn, in whose name it continued till 1760, when on failure of issue, it descended to Thomas Pigot, Esq. of Manchester, the heir-at-law, and was by him settled on Charles Wood, Esq., a captain in the Royal Navy, who received a mortal wound, Sept. 31, 1782, in an engagement between Sir Edward Hughes and a French Squadron, in the East

Indies. On his death, the manor of Bowling descended to his son, Sir Francis Lindley Wood, Bart, who sold it in 1815, to John Sturges, John Green Paley, and Thomas Mason, Esqs., and on the division of the property in 1821, that part of the estate on which the Hall is situated, along with the manor, and a chapel or chantry, in Bradford Church, attached to the mansion, fell to the share of Mr. Mason." *Jones' Views of the Seats, Mansions. Castles &c , London* 1829

(3) The date of 1660 is an important one in the history of the Colony, which was beginning to develope its resources in a wonderful degree. From the establishment of the Cromwellian government to the year 1660, the date of the restoration of Charles the Second, the Colonial authorities regulated substantially their own trade, which was confined, during the royal government, almost wholly to England, so far at least as Tobacco, our great staple, was concerned, and the planters dispatched their ventures to any foreign port that offered a profit upon them. They sent their lumber and naval stores to the West Indies, and to Madeira, and brought home bountiful supplies of rum, sugar molasses and Madeira wine of the first vintage. Hence, from this freedom of trade, there was an increase of population of the best sort, consisting of men of enterprise, capital, and industry. At a later date the tide was swelled by the friends of the Cromwellian government, who came over from political motives or necessities, and added to the industrious working population of the Colony.

(4) The marriage of Robert Bolling to Jane Rolfe shows very plainly that he early attained to comparative wealth and distinction. He was, at the time of his marriage twenty-nine years old, and had one son by his wife, who unfortunately died a year after her marriage The marriage of Pocahontas with John Rolfe or Rolphe, a name that comes from the same root as Ralph and Randolph, viz: *radulphus*, is one of the most interesting interludes in our early history, and deserves a passing remark. Rolfe, who was of Norman descent, and whose ancestor came over at the conquest with the Conqueror, was a scholar, well educated at one of the English universities, a man of pure morals and indeed a devout Christian. The specimens of his writings which have come down to us, speak

with equal force of his piety—which was an impelling motive to his marriage with Pocahontas, as he himself alleges—of his scholarship, and of his general benevolence. One of these letters may be seen in Bishop Meade's *Old Churches*, &c., (vol. I p 126) in which he urges that a desire for the Christian instruction of Pocahontas was one of his reasons for inter-marrying with the Indian princess; but there can be no doubt that her beauty, to say nothing of her personal worth and imperial dignity, was the principal reason. She must have been very beautiful to have won the heart of an Oxford scholar of independent circumstances at a time when the Indian race were regarded as savages and beyond the pale of the affections of a native of Europe. A description of Virginia from the pen of Rolfe, addressed to the King, may be found in the *Virginia Historical Register*, vol I. pp 102 *et seq*, and in the *Literary Messenger* for June 1839.

(5) Some of the descendants by this second marriage resided in Petersburg, and the surrounding country. They were generally possessed of large estates. One of them, Robert Bolling of Petersburg, owned a very large part of that town.

(6) Kippax—this place was also known as Farmingdale. The epitaph on Mr. Robert Bolling's tombstone there reads as follows: "Here lyeth interred, in hope of a joyful resurrection, the body of Robert Bolling, the son of John and Mary Bolling, of Allhallows, Barkin Parish, Tower Street, London. He was born the 26th of December, in the year of 1646, and came to Virginia, October the 2d, 1660, and departed this life the 17th day of July, 1709, aged sixty-two years six months, and twenty one dayes." The following history of the name of this place, is taken from a letter of John Randolph, of Roanoke written in 1832. 'The letter which I had previously received from you, bore date at or near Cawsons; and then P— was living at Kippax, alias Farmingdale or Farmingdell (as the romantic Mrs. Blodget — Corran, named it)-alias Smoky or Smoaky Lane, (as my grandfather used to call it:) but the true name is Kippax, called after the village of Kippax and Kippax Park, adjacent thereto, the seat of my maternal ancestors, the Blands, in the West Riding of York." [In some old letters, it is styled Smoaky Hall.]

Bland Papers vol. I, *p.* xxx. [A description of Kippax Park, and a history of the Bland family, will be found in *Jones' Views of Seats, &c.*]

(7) The death of Robert Bolling at the age of sixty-two suggests the fact that the early Colonists rarely reached the period of the Psalmist, and died before seventy. Although we have not such an amount of evidence as would establish this fact incontrovertibly, yet all the information that has reached us, and the nature of the case, favor such a conclusion. In forming an opinion on this subject a paper from the British Foreign Office, containing a list of all the emigrants from 1607 to 1625, may be consulted with profit. A partial publication of this document was made forty years ago in the papers; but a copy, which is in every respect full and authentic, is in the library of Mr Bancroft in manuscript; and this comparative shortness of life continued to be the case up to the revolution of 1776. With this last event it would seem that a new era began: and it is remarkable that most of the eminent men, who had arrived at mature age when the troubles that ended in the Revolution began, attained to seventy. George and Thomson Mason, Patrick Henry, Richard Henry Lee, Robert Carter Nicholas, and some others, died in the sixties, but Col. Richard Bland, Pendleton, Wythe, Paul Carrington, and a number of the younger friends of the Revolution, such as Jefferson, Madison, Monroe, Marshall, Brooke, and many others, went, some of them, far beyond seventy. The fact seems nearly certain, that human life has rather been prolonged than shortened since the Revolution.

(8) Most of the large estates accumulated by the early as well as by the late colonists were from the profits of mercantile transactions, and mechanical trades, practised in addition to farming, which supplied funds for investments in lands. It was not so common for the tobacco planter, who depended solely on his tobacco crop, to become very rich. That crop was so uncertain in its returns that it frequently failed to pay the expenses of the current year. But merchandising was more profitable, and many of the planters trained their slaves as carpenters, bricklayers, blacksmiths, &c, and contracted

to build dwelling-houses, churches, barns, &c. The old wooden structure, St. John's Church, on Church Hill, Richmond, which is celebrated for the remarkable display of Henry's eloquence on the proposition to put the Colony into a posture of defence in 1775, was built by one of the Randolphs, whose slaves did all the wood and brick work in its construction. The number and character of the merchants of the Colony, at the Revolution, may be seen in the names of the Mercantile Association, held in Williamsburg in 1770. (*Va. Hist. Reg*, III, 78) When the planters had a little money in hand, they instantly invested it in lands, the only source of speculation in the Colony, and laid the foundation of a family. These lands, which they took up by thousands of acres, were secured by the laws of entail and primogeniture, and remained in some families until the repeal of those acts by the General Assembly of the Commonwealth, some time after the revolution.

(9) The following notice of John Bolling and his residence, will be found in Col. Wm. Byrd's interesting account of the History of the Dividing Line between Virginia and North Carolina. He says: "At the end of 30 good Miles, we arrived in the Evening at Colo. Bolling's, where first, from a Primitive Course of Life, we began to relapse into Luxury. This gentleman lives within Hearing of the Falls of Appamatuck River, which are very Noisy whenever a Flood happens to roll a greater stream than ordinary over the Rocks." (*Byrd Papers* vol 1, p 193.)

(10) The Colonists brought over the vocabulary of King James' day, which was the vocabulary of Shakspeare, of Spencer, and of Raleigh, and, we may add, of Bacon also, and preserved it in its purity. As we had no accessions of population from any other quarter than England, and were engaged in agriculture that required no new words for its processes, it happened, in the progress of years, that we retained words that became obsolete in the parent country, and have been denounced subsequently as *Americanisms*, though a portion of the legacy brought over by our fathers. There are two words which have long been regarded as *Virginianisms*, but which were brought over by the Colonists, and preserved here, though lost in the mother country. We now say daily in

Virginia, and have said for two centuries and a half, that such a man was *raised* in such a place. Mr. Wirt introduced the word into his memoirs of Henry, and was laughed at for using it by the British writers and our own; but if the reader will turn to the life of Lord Herbert, of Cherbury, written by himself, and rescued from oblivion by the tutelary genius of Strawberry Hill, he will find the word. Lord Herbert lived between 1581 and 1641, that is, through a tract of time embracing Sir Walter Raleigh's settlement, and the death of Charles the First, and probably wrote his work in 1634, or thereabouts. On the second page of the London edition, the word "*raise*" is used in our Virginia sense; and the word "*tote*," which is properly *tolt* from *tollo*, was in common use at the English bar, from 1600 to the middle of the century, in the sense of lifting or removing a writ from one court to another; and thence applied to the lifting and carrying away any object whatever. (See the Glossographia of Blunt, edition of 1660.) The same may be said of other words, which, though they have slipped from the English tongue of modern times are retained by our own. Our only fault is, that we have retained with fidelity the legacy bequeathed to us by our ancestors. We did indeed add a few Indian words to our speech, such as hominy, chinquepin, cymblin, and such like; but these are well-known, and are a clear gain.

(11) The Kennons probably came over from England between 1660 and 1690, and settled somewhere in the interior, as did most of the families who came over from that time, readily accessible from the James; they in due time acquired property, became prominent in the counties, and obtained seats in the House of Burgesses. In 1736 William Kennon represented Henrico in the Assembly, having for his colleague, Richard Randolph. As every family has a favorite Christian name, so the name of Richard was that of the Kennons, who, by the way, were of the Norman branch of our race. The last Richard in the public service that we can recall, was the late Dr Richard Kennon, of the United States Navy, who entered that service, in which his two elder brothers were engaged, as a midshipman, soon after the close of the war of 1812, made several cruises, then studied medicine, and resigning his

office as midshipman, re-entered as assistant surgeon. He died about middle age. His elder brother George entered the United States Navy early, as assistant surgeon; became surgeon and resigned some years before his death. Another elder brother, a gentleman of fine personal appearance, became a captain in the Navy, and perished in the fatal explosion of the big gun of the Princeton frigate, when several other Virginians fell or narrowly escaped

(12) Richard Randolph was a grandson of William Randolph, of Turkey Island, who came over from England, between the years 1660 and 1675, accumulated a large estate, had a large family of sons and daughters, whom he educated well and richly endowed; he was the patriarch of his name and race in Virginia, and became a member of the House of Burgesses, of which he was chosen Speaker; was a member of the Council, and, it is believed, was for a short time, its President, as its senior member becomes in the casual absence of the Governor. He died in 1711, and was buried on his estate at Turkey Island, where his tomb-stone may still be seen; unfortunately the epitaph does not mention the date of his birth, and we can ascertain neither his age, which could not have been far from one or the other side of seventy, nor the date of his arrival in the Colony. All the Randolphs in the Colony were descended from him. By intermarriages during two centuries, the blood of this venerable patriarch runs in the veins of several thousand decendants, some of whom are utterly unconscious of the fact that they are connected with a family, which, in all the aspects of the past and present, may be pronounced the most distinguished race in the History of the Colony and the Commonwealth. It would consume a volume to write the history of the Randolphs, when it is considered that even in our own time, Thomas Jefferson, John Marshall, Edmund Randolph, Thomas Mann Randolph and John Randolph of Roanoke, were of the number. For the names and other particulars relating to the children of William Randolph, the patriarch, see Bishop Meade's *Old Churches*, Vol. I. p 138. We have already said that the original ancestor of the Randolphs came over to England with William the Conqueror, and that his name is included in the Roll

of Battle Abbey. [For a brief memoir of Edmund Randolph, see Appendix "A" to these notes.]

(13) The number of daughters of Robert Bolling shows how the name is not as numerous as that of many families who had fewer children, but those children sons, but whose descendants are not to be compared in point of numbers with those of the Bollings; and how, in the succession of generations, without the guidance of a well-known patronymic the tie of relationship is lost or forgotten. In relation to the Flemings, the reader must remember that there were two families of that name at the Revolution, who took an active part during the war The Fleming of the Convention of 1776, the honest and able Judge of the Court of Appeals, belonged to the family connected with the Bollings; but Col. William Fleming, who was of the Council in Mr Jefferson's gubernatorial term, was a Scotch physician, who came over under the auspices of Gov. Dinwiddie, settled in Augusta, as Augusta then was, was an officer at the battle of Point Pleasant, and was the ancestor of the Baxters, of the Vallley, of whom the former Attorney General of Virginia, Sidney Baxter, is one

(14) The fruitfulness of the families in the Colony deserves to be noted more especially as we have already observed that the annual average of the duration of human life, so far as such a fact can be inferred from the imperfect data in our possession, was less in the Colony than it has been in the Commonwealth. Seventeen, which was the number of Queen Anne's children, was not only reached frequently in the Colony but was often exceeded. It was rare to find two or three children only in a family of which both parents were living Queen Anne's number, as it was commonly called, prevailed from the sea-coast to the remotest settlements of Augusta, when Augusta stretched to the Mississippi. The family of the Tuckers of Norfolk illustrates the populousnesss of the household of the Colony. The venerable Colonel Tucker had eighteen grown children by one wife, living at the same time. It also appears that the children throve well during infancy, and that the mortality was more perceptible between thirty-five and sixty. This is recognizable in old graveyards as well as in written genealogies. Extreme old age was not usual, that is,

the number of each generation, between the ages of seventy and eighty, was less in proportion, so far as may be judged at this late day, than at present. Elderly men of wealth and leisure usually went off between sixty and sixty-five. Two things then existed in the Colony, which have almost, at least in the general opinion, disappeared in our time, and which are believed to have had some relationship to each other: Madeira wine, not the manufactured article of the present century, but the legitimate juice of the grape, was almost universally used, and used freely, by the better classes; and the gout, which affected the elderly people, most of those who were well to do in the world dying of that disease. It is the opinion of our physicians that gout is now a comparatively rare disease, but it well becomes them to reflect whether it was ever known in the annals of medicine that a disease, hereditary for ages in a race, had suddenly disappeared; and whether its supposed disappearance is anything more than a failure of the disease to show itself in its old and palpable manifestations.

(15) A seat in the House of Burgesses, like a seat in the British House of Commons, was the first object of ambition to the country gentleman, and whiskey, or native brandy, or West India Rum, was spent very freely at elections, which, unless in the case of a dissolution of the Assembly by the Governor, were held once in seven years only. Hence a member might serve twenty-eight years, and be elected but four times. This is the secret of that length of public service which has always existed in Virginia, as well since the elections were annual or biennial, as when they were septennial. While the young and ambitious frequently held seats in the House of Burgesses, the majority of the members, or, at all events, a very considerable proportion of them, were advanced in life, and the body from the restoration of Charles the Second to the date of the Revolution was never new.

But Mr. Bolling was also *County-Lieutenant*, an office borrowed from England, where it is held usually by a nobleman either of high rank, or of political influence. This officer was always styled colonel, was the organ of communication with the Governor and the Secretary of the Colony, commanded the Militia, and presided in the County Courts. He was appointed by the Governor with the advice of his Council, was generally the most prominent citizen, and held his office during good behavior, or the pleasure of the executive. His commission was always drawn out in due form.

(16.) This policy of slighting the daughters in the division of the patrimonial property was borrowed from England, and is one of the most unpleasant incidents in our colonial customs. The land, or the larger portion of it, was almost invariably given with the home estate, and its equipments in furniture, plate, pictures and general outfit, to the eldest son, and entailed upon him. A negro quarter, not unfrequently without a good dwelling, was bestowed on the younger sons, while a negro or two, too often made up the patrimony of a daughter. This circumstance alone should make us rejoice at the abolition of the law of entails and of the right of the first-born male of a family. To turn a lovely and accomplished daughter, who had been bred in luxury, from the patrimonial dwelling with only the clothes upon her back as a fortune, and a maid or two in her train, seems revolting to every sense of delicacy and justice. From this custom, which by the way flows inevitably from the distinction of ranks in a country, arose those negotiations about marriage settlements, which are immemorial in England, and by which a father seeks to provide for a daughter's future support out of her husband's property, and to keep his own substance for his sons. Hence the large number of unmarried women in the upper classes of British society.

(17.) Thomas Bolling lived at Cobb's, in Chesterfield county, and was buried there about the beginning of the present century. He was a man of fine form and appearance, of pleasing manners, and amiable disposition. He was for many years a justice of the peace of his county, and except in the discharge of the moderate duties of that office led a life of entire ease and leisure.

(18.) John Bolling, the second of that name, lived in Chesterfield county, and died there towards the close of the last century. His characteristics were in strong contrast with those of his wife, who was a very refined lady. He was addicted to strong drink, and in consequence of that propensity was familiarly called "The old Indian.'

(19.) Robert Bolling the author of this memoir.

(20.) The small number of negroes, less than two hundred, of all ages, and the large number of plantations, fifteen or eighteen in number, explain how easily the planters were overwhelmed in debt, as almost all of them were. These quarters, even in successful years, did little more than pay the necessary expenses of cultivation, and three or four bad years served to plunge the planter in debt, whose main resource was to slice off a part of the estate to pay wages of overseers. These overseers, who were active, industrious and skillful, set zealously to work on their own freeholds, founded families, became prosperous, and rose either in themselves or their children to the best stations in society. They composed that middle class which in almost every free country is the most virtuous, the most useful in peace or war, yet making a slight impression on the page of history, as history is too usually written. In looking at the number of slaves mentioned in the will of a colonial testator, it must be kept in mind that up to the date of the Revolution there were white men called Redemptioners, who were bound to the planters for a term of years, and who worked in the field, and often at some trade during their term of service, and these were seldom mentioned in wills, which were often written long before the death of the testator, and which could not provide beforehand for a class of men whose terms were expiring every year.

(21.) Mr. Bolling judged rightly about the interest which would be felt in future times respecting the details of the race of the first and earlier settlers of Virginia, and deserves credit for what he has left us about his family. While there is hardly a doubt that many of our earlier and later settlers were descended from ancient and honorable families in England, the want of an accurate record in determining particulars is felt in the case of all. The recent disclosures in the case of the Washingtons show this very plainly.* At the pre-

---

* See Appendix B.

sent day no contribution to history in our modern conception of the word and work is more valuable or interesting, not only to a particular family, but to all others, than a correct genealogical table running back two or more centuries, especially if its colonial delegation be full and fully delineated. In ascertaining the elements of a population genealogical records are of the greatest value to a modern historian. Ancient portraits, if the term ancient can be applied to a period of two or three centuries, have an inestimable value in ascertaining the character and form of an ancestor as well as the state of the arts; and it would be a good office to hunt up and record the portraits of the Virginians of the seventeenth and eighteenth centuries, which still exist in Virginia. The oldest and most consecutive series of family portraits now known to us in Virginia belongs to the heirs of the late Col. Burwell B. Moseley, of Norfolk, Va. These, we believe, reach back to the date of the Protectorate. A portrait of Robert Carter, of Corotoman, is still preserved at Shirley, on James river, or was there before our recent troubles. The portraits of the Newtons, of Norfolk, painted by Durand, run back to 1713, and are in the possession of their worthy descendant Tazewell Taylor, Esq. The Moseley and the Newton portraits embrace a longer continuous period than any other collection that we can now call to mind. The Wright, the Balfour, and the Walke portraits present a field of observation, but are confined to the eighteenth century. A *catalogue raisonnée* of the old portraits of Virginia, with full descriptions of the originals, the names of the artists, and their present locality, would be a valuable contribution to our historical literature. The period of the Revolution is very deficient in portraits. Any intelligent young historical student, who has a summer to spare for literary recreations, and would undertake to prepare such a paper as we have pointed out, could easily obtain such information as might facilitate his labors and make them pleasant.

(22.) Varina, which was settled early, is now the property of Mr. Albert Aiken, and during the late war it was known as Aiken's landing, where the prisoners were exchanged. It still retains its ancient name, and was so called from the resemblance of the tobacco raised there to that made at Varina in Spain. So popular was the tobacco raised in our Virginia Varina, that in foreign quotations Varina was used as the synonyme of tobacco. Governor Thomas Mann Randolph inherited this estate, and resided on it during the winter months for several years.

(23.) The name of Robert Carter Nicholas is truly venerable, and has a religious sanctity about it which is peculiar to itself, and which should endear it to all, especially to his numerous descendants in Virginia and Kentucky. But when young Bolling entered his office, Col. Nicholas, as he was then called, was comparatively young, had been and was a member of the House of Burgesses—and ten years later, say 1766, was, on the separation of the office of Treasurer from that of the Speaker, elected by the Assembly the first independent Treasurer of the Colony, at least in latter years. This office he filled till 1776, when in consequence of the incompatibility of the offices of a member of the House of Delegates and Treasurer under the new constitution, as he preferred to remain in the House, he resigned the Treasury in those words which found a place on the journal, and which Mr Madison, who was present and heard them when uttered, was fond of repeating: "I leave the office of Treasurer," said Colonel Nicholas, "with clean hands—certainly with empty ones." He was a member of all the early Conventions that preceded the Commonwealth, was elected a Judge of the General Court under the new constitution, and died under sixty at his farm in Hanover in 1780, while his country was involved in the darkest clouds of the Revolution. Among his sons may be mentioned George, who was one of the ablest statesmen who composed the Convention of 1788, and who emigrated to Kentucky, where his authority was as great as it had been in Virginia; and Wilson Cary, who was a member of the Convention of 1788 also, a member of both houses of Congress, and Governor of Virginia, and lies buried in the graveyard of Monticello. A fine portrait of Gov. Nicholas may be seen on the walls of Edgehill, the seat of our venerable fellow-citizen, Col. Thomas Jefferson Randolph, whose wife is a daughter of the Governor. It was taken when he was between forty-five and fifty, is well executed, and is regarded a good likeness.

(24.) The following article from the "notes and queries" column of the Baltimore Leader, of October 3d, 1868, in reply to a question by the editor will inform those who do not understand this allusion:

"THE PASTOR FIDO OF GUARINI.

Guarini was the contemporary of Tasso, and died at Venice in 1612. The "Pastor Fido" (Faithful Shepherd) was first represented in 1585 The plot of this drama is as follows:

Arcadia, under the displeasure of Diana, for more than a century, is compelled to sacrifice a young virgin annually.

> "Che duo semi del ciel congiunga Amore:
> E di donna infadel l'antico errore
> L'alta pieta d'un Pastor Fido ammende."
> *Act I*, *Scene 2.*

> "Till two of race divine be joined by Love,
> And high devotion of a faithful swain
> Expiate one woman's long and fatal error."

Silvio, sprung from Pan, and *Amaryllis*, from Hercules, are those only by whose union the Arcadians hope for release by fulfilment of the oracle. They are betrothed, but *Silvio* is insensible to the charms of *Amaryllis*, as well as of *Dorinda*, who loves him fondly *Mirtillo*, a poor shepherd of obscure birth, loves *Amaryllis*, who returns his affection. *Corisca*, secretly attached to *Mirtillo*, prompted by jealousy, charges the loss of chastity against *Amaryllis*, a shepherdess, subjected to Vestal laws in Arcadia, and she is adjudged to death *Mirtillo* offers to die in her stead, and, at the very moment of sacrifice, his foster-father appears and proves him to be the brother of *Silvio*, and descended of the gods. The oracle is fulfilled. The faithful shepherd is united in love to one, like himself, of celestial origin, and Arcadia released from the dreadful annual sacrifice of blood *Silvio*, having accidentally wounded the loving *Dorinda*, is softened by her charms, and weds her. *Corisca* repents and receives pardon, and all are happy."

(25.) It is amusing to see the means of designating the father of President Jefferson at the time the Bolling genealogy was written. A sister of the author of the Declaration of Independence may now be known without circumlocution. She was a daughter of Jane Randolph, and formed another tie of relationship between the Bollings and the Randolphs. We are sorry to say that we have not been able to ascertain any existing portrait or miniature of Jane Randolph, or of her husband Peter Jefferson, who, like the Randolphs, came from the Norman stock.

(26.) The translator of Homer, the author of the Virginia Reports bearing his name, and the father of our worthy fellow-citizen, George Wythe Munford, Esq., William Munford, Esq., was the son of the Robert Munford of the text. Robert Munford was a soldier of the Revolution, attained the rank of Colonel, and resided in Mecklenburg county, in this State. He devoted his leisure hours to eloquence and poetry, and published a volume of "Poems and Compositions in Prose on several occasions," in the latter part of the year 1798. It contains a poem on St. Clair's defeat, several happy translations of some of the odes of Horace, a versifying of Ossian's address to the Sun and to the Moon, of the Songs of Selma and the Battle of Lora, and an oration delivered at Williamsburg, on the 4th of July, 1793, and other things in prose and verse. It is an octavo of about two hundred pages. But the name of this worthy patriot has been lost in that of his son, William, whom we have already mentioned as the translator of Homer. He was educated at William and Mary College, studied law, resided in Mecklenburg, and afterwards in Richmond, prepared several volumes of the Virginia Reports separately and in conjunction with Hening, and devoted his spare moments to the muses. He pronounced a very effective eulogy on the death of Chancellor Wythe, which may be seen in one of the earliest volumes of the Richmond Enquirer, and which has a high value as asserting on the authority of the speaker that Wythe died in the full belief of Christianity—an important fact, as the reverse has been stated on high authority in our own times. But his translation of Homer is his great work, and has been pronounced by that accomplished scholar and most excellent man, the late President Felton, of Harvard University, the best translation of the Grecian bard. When Munford undertook the task, the existing translations of Homer were those of Ogilvie, Chapman, Pope and Cowper.

Since the date of President Felton's opinion, it is proper to say that two translations of the Iliad have appeared from high sources in England. Mr. Munford was long a member of the House of Delegates, and afterwards its clerk. He died in Richmond on the 21st of June, 1825, at the early age of forty-nine. He was succeeded in his office as clerk of the House of Delegates by his son Col. G. Wythe Munford, as above stated, who filled the office without contestation and with great ability for many years, when he resigned it to become the Secretary of the Commonwealth, in which position his intimate knowledge of the men and things of Virginia was of vast service to the Executive. This office he held until the close of the war in 1865, when the Legislature, elected under influences opposed to those who had taken part with the Confederacy, removed him. We rejoice to say that he still lives, residing on a farm of his own in Gloucester county, Va., and has given a brilliant sample of his powers of oratory in a discourse delivered in Richmond since the war.

This family seems to have possessed for many generations what has been sarcastically called "the barbarous virtue of hospitality." Frequent mention is made of Col. Munford, [in all probability the father of the young man named in the text,] and his liberality in supplying the gentlemen engaged in running the dividing line between Virginia and North Carolina, with provisions and other comforts by Col Byrd — [*Byrd Papers, Vol. I., pp. 87, 179, 185, 193.*]

(27.) The schools of Wakefield, in Yorkshire, were evidently very popular with the people of Virginia; and Mr. Bolling's contemporaries there included some men who afterwards made their marks in American history. Theodorick Bland was there from 1753 to 1758, and Richard Henry Lee left a school at the same place in 1752.—[*Bland Papers, Vol. I. p. xv.*]

(28.) John Blair was a relative of young Bolling, John Bolling having married a daughter of Archibald Blair. Young Blair was at this time in his twenty-third year, had passed with honor through the classes of William and Mary College, was studying law in the Temple, and was a very fair representative of the educated youth of the Colony. He was about five feet ten inches in height, of an erect and imposing stature, with a noble forehead, blue eyes, a well-formed nose not deficient in size, hair inclining to be red, and an expression of sweetness and gravity which adhered to him through life. He soon after returned to Virginia, engaged in the practice of law, became a member of the House of Burgesses, and a member of all the early Conventions, and of the Virginia Convention of 1788, as well as of the General Federal Convention which formed the Federal Constitution. His name and that of Madison are the only names from Virginia, excepting that of Washington, attached to that instrument. On the formation of the new State judiciary he was placed on the bench by the side of Wythe and Pendleton, and on the establishment of the Federal Courts he was made an associate justice of the Supreme Court of the United States, the duties of which office he performed until his death in the city of Williamsburg, on the 31st of August, 1800, at the age of sixty-eight. His manners, formed in the school of Fauquier and Botetourt, and in the refined society of the ancient metropolis, where his name and memory are still living in the hospitable mansion of one of his descendants, and in the hearts of all, were marked by high-bred courtesy and gentleness; and he preserved to the last that strict attention to his dress which was the characteristic of the colonial regime. A beautiful, enamelled miniature of the face of this fine old patriot is before us as we trace these lines. The hair has not yet lost entirely the reddish tinge of his earlier years, though a more ample forehead attracts attention, and the placid gentleness of youth still adorns his venerable features. Like all the patriots of the field and the forum of the Revolution, he has no hair upon his face; he is attired in a blue coat, with a high collar, a white vest buttoning to the throat, and a white cravat without a collar. The name of the artist is unknown to us, though it is probably the work of the elder Peale, and has a delicacy of touch beyond the reach of Durand, to whose brush we owe so many of the surviving portraits of the colonial era. His descendant, William S. Peachy, Esq., of Williamsburg, has a full sized portrait of the Judge. Judge Blair was descended from a brother of the Commissary, James Blair, as are all those who bear the name in Virginia, with the exception of those who are sprung from the Rev John D. Blair, of Richmond, in the olden time And we may mention here that a full sized portrait of the Commissary and one of his wife still exist, and are at present in the parlor of the President of William and Mary College, suspended near the portrait of the celebrated Robert Boyle, of whose charity the Brafferton house in the college yard still exists as a memorial The portrait of Boyle, which represents two-thirds of the figure, was the gift of the Earl of Burlington to the College, and is a fair work of art, and in good preservation. It has been in the possession of the college for a century and more. Whoever is familiar with the office of tracing the descent of families for one or two hundred years will be struck with the similarity of the characteristics, modified more or less by the times, that adhere to its members. A blessing seems always to have rested on the name of Blair. The venerable head of the family in Virginia, the Rev. James Blair, the Commissary of the Bishop of London for Virginia—an office of the same class and dignity as that of the present Bishop of the diocese of the Episcopal Church in this State—came over in 1685, after having withdrawn from Scotland to England, in consequence of the religious turmoils that distracted his native land. Peace and good will to men, and a love of letters, composed his motto, which he illustrated by a series of discourses on the sermon of our Saviour on the Mount and by his obtaining from King William, in 1692, the charter of William and Mary College. This old man lived in the full enjoyment of his faculties to August the 1st, 1743, when at the age of eighty-eight he died, and was buried at Jamestown, where a beautiful tomb, on which was recorded an elegant Latin inscription, and which we saw in its perfect state in 1835, was erected to his memory by his nephews, who were also his heirs. This tomb had a singular fate. A tree which grew up by its side seventy or eighty years after its erection, over-lapped the flat top stone, and bore it from the shell several feet in the air. In this position the stone was broken by some reckless young men. He died childless, bequeathing his books to his darling college. Just as his sun went down, there arose one of his name and race, a nephew, whom he had educated, John Blair, who succeeded the Commissary as a member of the Council, and became also the President of the body, as his uncle had been before him, and displayed in the administration of its duties a wisdom and clemency that now brighten his name on the page of history. He died before the Revolution, but not before his son, the Judge John Blair of the text, had a seat in the House of Burgesses, and was a prominent lawyer at the bar of the General Court. This son died while a justice of the Supreme Court of the United States in 1800, being one of three men of the same name and blood who had filled continuously the highest civil and religious offices of the Colony and Commonwealth, and of the Union, from 1687 to 1800, a period of one hundred and fifteen years. During the present century it may be safely said that those who have borne the name and the blood of the patriarch in their veins, if not conspicuous in the bustling arena of politics, have graced the walks of professional and domestic life. It may be observed also that, though the venerable Commissary died without children, the College which he founded has ever been an object of affection to those who own his name and his blood. Three times has the main structure of the College been destroyed by fire. The old president, as he superintended the first building, so he presided over the arrangements for the erection of the second; and when that second edifice was burned in 1858, the chairman of the building committee on the part of the visitors bore his name; and when that building was destroyed during the late war, of the three members of the committee appointed by the visitors to superintend the erection of the new structure, one of them, who was also chairman, bore the name, and another was the lineal descendant of the nephew of the first president. Thus for one hundred and seven years has the name of Blair been connected with the building of the main edifice of William and Mary College.

The question arises to which branch of the mingled races that make up the British people do the Blairs belong? Whether to the Saxon, the Norman, or the Celtic? If we derive the races from the names which they bear, they would seem to be Celtic, for Blair is a common Celtic word, signifying an open space, and thence, from the pugnacious qualities of the Scotch people, it came to mean a field of battle. But in this case it is plainly a delusive test, as there was no sept or clan of Blair; and it is universally known that the lowland Scotch are almost entirely sprung from the Anglo-Saxons, who at an early date penetrated to the base of the highlands, and more especially after the Norman invasion; and at the origin of surnames, a comparatively recent period, took, after the English fashion, the names of the places near which they dwelt. We thus lean to the opinion that the race is Saxon.

The same remark about the hereditary traits and tastes of families will apply to the Randolphs. William Randolph, of Turkey Island, from whom all the Virginia Randolphs spring, came over to the colony about a quarter of a century earlier than Commissary Blair; and, like nearly all of the early colonists, however well they were connected in England, was in narrow circumstances. His first object was to acquire a competent fortune, and to marry a wife whose relationship in the Colony and in England was equal to his own. As soon as these objects were accomplished, as if inspired with a desire to maintain the reputation which his ancestors in England and Scotland had enjoyed immemorially, and especially in the reign of Elizabeth, he entered the House of Burgesses, of which he was Speaker during one session, was in due time chosen of the Council, and, like James and John Blair, Sr., became the President of the body, and was *ex-officio*, in the absence of the royal representative, the Governor of the Colony. He had a large number of children, and educated his sons as carefully as if he lived in the shadow of Eton or of Harrow. His son John, who had been educated at William and Mary, and at the Temple, was soon at the head of the colonial bar, was a member of the House of Burgesses, was Attorney General, and finally Speaker of the House of Burgesses and Treasurer, and was the only person in the Colony, from the settlement at Jamestown to the Declaration of Independence, who received from the King the dignity of knighthood. He too educated his two sons with all the skill and care that money and talents could command. His eldest son, Peyton, studied law, entered the House of Burgesses, was chosen Attorney General, was elected Speaker of the House of Burgesses, was sent to Congress, and became its President. The second son of Sir John also became Attorney General, and continued in the office till the Revolution. His son, Edmund, succeeded him as Attorney General, under the new Constitution of the State, and became the first Attorney General of the United States and Secretary of State. Thus William Randolph, and four of the descendants of one branch of his family, filled the highest offices of the Colony, of the Commonwealth, and of the Federal Union, from 1660 to near 1800, a period of one hundred and forty years; and let us say in passing that these eminent men were indebted for their success to their own talents and accomplishments. We may add farther that during that interval of nearly a century and a half other branches of the family, bearing the name or the blood of the race, were filling high offices in the country, and some of them still more exalted offices than were filled by the knight and his sons, and the same may be said of the race to the present hour.

(29.) See note 34 for supposed rectification of this date.

(30.) The Waller of the text was Benjamin Waller, who was then a practising lawyer, but subsequently became clerk of the General Court, one of the most important and most honorable offices in the Colony. Few of those who reached the present century could recall him, as he was when Bolling entered his office. He was then in his thirty-ninth year, was tall and well-formed, his complexion brilliant but tinged with that deep tropical hue, which is still seen in his descendants. He was the son of Edmund Waller, who was probably a descendant of the poet Waller, whose full name he bore, in the third or fourth degree, and emigrated to the Colony about the beginning of the eighteenth century. His son, Benjamin, the person named in the text was probably born in Williamsburg and educated at William and Mary College. At the breaking out of the Revolution he had long been clerk of the General Court and held a high position as a lawyer and gentleman. When the Constitution was formed in 1776 he was appointed chief of the Court of Admiralty, and as such was a Judge of the first Court of Appeals. He was distinguished by his knowledge of the law of Admiralty; and even when clerk of the General Court, before the Revolution, he was often consulted in marine cases by the Governor and Council, who composed that body. He died in 1780, at the age of seventy. But this excellent man, who is the ancestor of the present Wallers of Virginia, is now mainly known as the maternal grand-father of Littleton Waller Tazewell, whose earlier years were spent under his roof, which, by the way, is still to be seen near the site of the old capitol, in Williamsburg, and who received his first instructions from his lips. The Wallers derive their name from the French La Valliere, and the original ancestors probably came over from Normandy to England. Lower, in his work on surnames, which is very inaccurate and superficial, derives the name from the Anglo-Saxon *waller-wente*, signifying foreign men, strangers. So that either derivation points beyond England as the cradle of the race. In the name of Littleton Waller Tazewell may be found a singular union of the Saxon and the Norman. The name of Littleton, which Gov. Tazewell derived from his great-great grandfather, Col. Southey Littleton, of Accomack, is Saxon; and it is worth noting that our late distinguished fellow-citizen could trace his lineage through the Littletons to the great lawyer, whose name, inseparably connected with that of Sir Edward Coke's, will be fresh as long as the law of England endures. The name of Waller, as already said, is most probably Norman; and that of Tazewell is certainly so. Judge Waller was buried in the family graveyard, which is on the estate still owned by his grandson, near Williamsburg Va.

(31.) The following passage in the memoir of Theodorick Bland, prefixed to the Bland papers, would seem to prove that there was some slight foundation for this report.

"In the year 1759 young Bland resided at Liverpool for the purpose of attending the infirmary of that town as a student of physic. About the year 1761 he repaired to Edinburgh, to pursue the study of that profession at the University there * * * His application, however, seems not to have monopolized his time so exclusively as to prevent him from falling into a love affair—the object of which was a Miss

Anne Miller, a young lady from Virginia, who was then in Edinburgh The scheme was strenuously opposed by his father and his friend Dr. Fothergill, and was shortly afterwards abandoned." [*Bland Papers. Vol. I. p.* XVII.]

(32) This lady's brief existence after her marriage elicited an eloquent tribute to her many virtues by her husband, from which we make the following extract:

"I addressed in the Bloom of Life, and became Husband to —— Lavinia Her age was fifteen, her Person graceful, her Soul Spotless as the new fallen Snow A native Candor and amiable Simplicity dignified her Action: her black eyes (full of Complacency) and benevolent Features resembled those of the immortal Gods, contemplating the *Sons of Virtue*. Her innocent Heart was mine and the humble Fair one esteemed—even my Love a Compensation · Her excellent Qualities rivetted her to my Soul. and we —— were happy

The rising Sun, whose Rays of Gold and Vermillion decorate the Eve of Morning, beheld our Happiness. its meridian Beams beheld us happy: and when the starry-mantled Night O'erspread her sable Canopy, the Day was indeed obscured · but our Felicity lost not of its Brightness. —— * * * * *

How oft, with united Hands and Hearts glowing with mutual Fondness, did the closing Day invite us to yonder Rivulet! The gentle Ripple of the Current, the little Fishes, gliding to the setting Sun, like animated Diamonds in liquid Chrystal: its verdant Borders, enamelled with Flowers ·—the solemn murmurings of the Forest, and lively Harmony of its retiring People, united Pleasure and variety. My lovely Girl was pleased: and her Pleasure was doubly mine

But alas! lofty Groves, feathered Warblers, limpid Rivulets, their scaly People and painted Margins delight not me With my beloved departed are their Charms: her Finger sheweth not their Beauties: her Lips of Roses move not in their Praise.

Thou art departed, my Beloved: departed to Bliss eternal. The World was unworthy thine Excellence: myself unworthy so sacred a Deposit."—"*Miscellanies · By R. Bolling—* 1764 —*ms volume.*

(33.) In a paper read before the Virginia Historical Society, [date not given] by Wyndham Robertson, Esq , the author proves conclusively that the true date of the marriage of Pocahontas should be set down on the 5th of April, 1614. [*See Virginia Historical Reporter, Vol. II., Part 1, 1860, p 67*]

(34) The following letter, which was sent to Conway Robinson Esq , by the gentleman to whom it was addressed, contains information which seems to fix the date of the death of the Princess Pocahontas:

"MANYTOWN, 5th May, 1849.

My Dear Sir.—The within extract, from the Parish Register of Burials, in the Parish of Gravesend, in the County of Kent, I examined, with the original, at the time the extract was made, the termination of the word Wrothe is rather obscure, but I think that the abbreviation was meant for a final e.

The date, 1616, is the correct year, but according to the computation of the Historical year, it is 1617.

I am, my dear sir,
Yours very truly,
CLEM T. SMYTHE."

CHARLES WYKEHAM, MARTIN, ESQ , M P.,
Leeds Castle, Kent

"1616
March 21 —Rebecca Wrothe wyffe of
Thomas Wrothe gent. A Virginia
Lady borne was buried in the
Chauncell"

Gravesend church having been destroyed by fire in 1727—if there had been any monument it was then destroyed

[For a discussion of the questions which suggest themselves in regard to the spelling of the name, and other matters connected therewith, *See Virginia Historical Register, volume II, 1849, page 187.*]

(35.) John Rolph, has, like all other men who have married famous women, become better known as the husband of Pocahontas, than for any merits of his own. He was a prominent useful, and enterprising gentleman; the first white man who engaged in the cultivation of tobacco; a well informed writer on subjects connected with the Colony of Virginia, and one whose character and services would have reflected credit upon any age and country. We had prepared a memoir for insertion in this note, but other matter having unexpectedly swelled the work beyond our first intentions, we have concluded to retain it for a more appropriate place in a work on the descendants of Pocahontas, which will be printed as soon as the materials for it are properly prepared.

(36.) A son of Robert Bolling of Chellowe, was a candidate for Congress in the Prince Edward district in 1799, with John Randolph and Clement Carrington as competitors. He was a man of a high spirit and bearing. Mr. Randolph was elected.

(37) Two volumes of his writings are still extant. One measuring seven and a quarter by four and three-quarter inches, and containing 176 pages, is now the property of Thomas Bolling, Sr of Bolling's Island, in Goochland county, Va. It is bound in boards, with a back of Russia leather, and lettered "Miscellanies," on the inside of the cover is the book plate of Robert Bolling, containing the Bolling arms, described in Burke's "General Armory" as "Sable, an in escutcheon within in orle of martlets argent," and, Mr Bolling being the third son, bore the appropriate badge i. e , a five pointed star in the upper part of the shield, technically styled, in what Dr Johnson calls "the barbarous jargon of heraldry," a mullet in the chief for difference; in place of supporters, the shield is ornamented with borders from classical subjects; a photographed copy of the book-plate forms the vignette to this work. The title page reads:

"A Collection
of
diverting Anecdotes,
Bons-Mots, and other
Trifling Pieces,
by
R Bolling, Jr.,
1764"

The title was evidently written during the first year of his married life, when he did not anticipate the blow to his happiness which fell upon him so suddenly, and which elicited from his pen, [in addition to such articles as Anecdote of Sir Wm. Gooch, Noveletta, Neanthe, an heroic tragic-comic tale; Epitaph on a lap-dog,] the "Funeral oration in memory of Mrs. Mary Bolling," from which a passage is quoted in note 32. The other volume, (measuring twelve inches by six inches, and containing 230 pages,) is full bound in Russia leather, and has two title pages: the first reading:

"Pieces Concerning Vineyards,
&
their establishment in Virginia,
&c.

"Dulce periculum est,
O Lenace, sequi, Deum.
Cingentem, viridi tempora pampino,—*Hor.*

By R Bolling, of Chellowe."

The first part contains four articles which the writer informs us were published in the Virginia Gazette, in 1773.

The second part is entitled

"A
sketch of
Vine Culture
for Pennsylvania, Maryland, Virginia and the Carolinas,
compiled by
R Bolling, Jr."

The initials of his name being in each instance united in the form of a monogram. A writer in the Historical Magazine for September, 1860, describes this volume, and gives an account of its rescue when on its way to a paper mill in Worcester, Mass. During the same year it was purchased from a book store in New York by the editor, and is now in his possession.

Both of these volumes contain articles in prose and poetry, and in the latter is a "Song from Chiabrera," set to music. Both of the books are written in a very plain and beautiful handwriting.

(38.) Col. Theodoric Bland, of Cawsons, Sr., was the father of Mrs. Randolph, afterwards Mrs. Tucker, the mother of the orator of Roanoke. It occurred to us at first, that the Theodoric Bland of the text was Col. Theodoric Bland, Jr., a son of the former, who was educated as a physician in Edinburg, became a soldier during the Revolution, as did Mercer and Fleming, who were also physicians; travelled in Europe, having John Wilkes as a companion for a time; and was a member of Congress under the Federal Constitution, dying while attending that body in New York, on the first of June, 1790, at the age of forty-eight. But Robert Bolling died some time before the Revolution, and Col. Bland, Sr., was living at the date of that event.

We have not noticed in detail the Beverly mentioned in the text, because we were unable to identify the particular individual; and because, in the notes to the Rose Diary, (see appendix C,) the genealogy of the family is given in some detail. The reader may consult page 481, of the second volume of Bishop Meade's Old Churches for some account of the family, which is Saxon, as the name of Beverly comes not from Belvoir, as some would take it, but from Beaver and ley, the place of the Beaver. It is one of our earliest and most honored families and is particularly entitled to historical notice, on account of Robert Beverly, the author of the history of Virginia.

It may be observed, in closing these notes, on a topic, intimately connected with genealogy, that is, the length of life in the Colony, that not a Bolling mentioned in the text, as far as we can learn, ever lived beyond the age of seventy. The same may be said of the Randolphs, with whom the Bollings inter-married. As we have already said, there is no evidence that the ancestor, William Randolph, of Turkey Island, went beyond that age, if he reached it, which he may have done, and *he* was born in England. His son, Sir John, died in the bloom of his age, and was buried in a vault in the chapel of

William and Mary College: but as his coffin was not encased in lead, hardly a vestige of it, (except the metal handles which being of silver, were stolen with similar articles in the vault, while the College was occupied by Federal troops during the late war,) or of the remains, existed, when examined about fifteen years ago. His two eminent sons died long before seventy. Peyton, the elder, the first President of Congress, died of paralysis at the house of a friend with whom he was dining, in Philadelphia, in 1775, under sixty. John, the brother of Peyton, the last Attorney-General of the Colony, who adhered to the British side, and withdrew to England, where he died, was hardly more than sixty or sixty-two. The leaden coffins of these two able brothers may still be seen in their respective vaults in the chapel of William and Mary, adjoining each other, and the vault of their father. Edmund Randolph, the son of John, died at sixty-two: and *his* son died under sixty. John Randolph, of Roanoke, reached sixty, but his elder brother, Richard, died between thirty and forty. The father of John Randolph, of Roanoke, also died at the age of thirty, or nearly so. The late Mr. Richard Randolph, the depository of the lore of his race, probably reached seventy; but with this exception, if exception it be, I have not heard of or seen a Randolph above seventy, except that noble representative of the family, the present Col. Thomas Jefferson Randolph, of Edgehill. The height of Col. Randolph, which exceeds that of all his paternal progenitors, and which he derives from his great-grandfather, Peter Jefferson, the father of the President, is six feet four inches and a half, in his stocking feet. He is large in graceful proportion to his height, treads the floor with the elasticity of five-and-twenty, and is seventy-six years old. He is descended from the races of Powhatan, Peter Jefferson, and William Randolph, of Turkey Island, and their blended blood could not flow in worthier veins. *Serus redeas in cœlo.* And of the other names mentioned in the genealogy we do not know of one who lived beyond seventy, excepting the Commissary, who reached eighty-eight, but *he* was born abroad. President Blair his nephew, may have been seventy, but not more; and his son, Judge John, was only sixty-eight at his decease. It seems at present to be the case at the sea-side, that the longest livers are those who, having been born abroad, and attained to manhood on their native soil, emigrated to this country, and were prosperous in their affairs. This has been particularly the case in Norfolk, where there is living (March 1869) a citizen, who was born in Ireland, and who, at the age of manhood, emigrated to Norfolk, where he has since resided, and prospered, and is now over ninety-three He walks from his house to the business part of the city, a distance of half a mile, attends to his various affairs, and returns home on foot. There is also a lady of Norfolk who is over ninety six, and has sometimes in her house five generations of her family. Her health and faculties are good, and her memory of recent events is as faithful as that of her children. She is, we believe, a native of Norfolk. We know, in the Valley of Virginia, an estimable lady, who entered her ninety-seventh year on the thirteenth of September last. But the greatest instance of advanced age within our personal observation, is that of Capt. Labibrush, of the British army, who, having been born in London, wished to spend his latter years in this country. He retains all his faculties, breakfasts, dines, and sups abroad, makes calls on his friends, and, at the age of *one hundred and three years*, actually goes a shopping with the ladies. He was visited by the Prince of Wales on his visit to New York, and was offered promotion on condition of his returning to England, but fearing a change at his advanced age, he declined the offer of the Prince. He is still living (March, 1869)

"Cawsons, situated on a commanding promontory, near the mouth of Appomattox River, was the family seat of Colonel Theodoric Bland, Sr., of Prince George. After winding amidst its woody islands, around the base of this hill, the river spreads out into a wide bay: and, together with the James, into which it empties, makes towards the north and east a magnificent water prospect, embracing in one view Shirley, the seat of the Carters, Bermuda Hundred, with its harbor and ships; City Point, and other places of less note In the midst of this commanding scene, the old mansion house reared its ample proportions, and, with its offices and extended wings, was not an unworthy representative of the Baronial days in which it was built—when Virginia Cavaliers, under the title of gentlemen, with their broad domain of virgin soil, and long retinue of servants, lived in a style of elegance and profusion, not inferior to the Barons of England, and dispensed a hospitality which more than half a century of sub-division, exhaustion and decay, has not entirely effaced from the memory of their impoverished descendants.

"At Cawson's scarcely a vestige now remains of former magnificence. The old mansion was burnt down many years ago. Here and there a solitary out-dwelling, which escaped the conflagration, like the old servants of a decayed family, seem to speak in melancholy pride of those days, when it was their glory to stand in the shadow of loftier walls and reflect back their loud revelry—when

> 'The misletoe hung in the castle hall,
> The holly branch shone on the old oak wall;
> And the Baron's retainers were blithe and gay,
> And keeping their Christmas holiday'

The serpentine paths, the broad avenues, and smooth gravel, the mounds, the green turf, and the shrubbery of extended pleasure grounds, are all mingled with the vulgar sod. The noble outlines of nature are still there; but the handiwork of man has disappeared.

"In a letter to his friend F. S Key dated March 20th, 1814, John Randolph says: 'A few days ago I returned from a visit to my birth place the seat of my ancestors on one side—the spot where my dear and honored mother was given in marriage, and where I was ushered in this world of woes The sight of the broad waters seemed to renovate me. I was tossed in a boat, during a row of three miles across James river, and sprinkled with the spray that dashed over her. The days of my boyhood seemed to be renewed: but at the end of my journey I found desolation and stillness as of death; the fires of hospitality long since quenched; the parish church, associated with my earliest and tenderest recollections, tumbling to pieces, not more from natural decay than sacrilegious violence' What a spectacle does our lower country present! Deserted and dismantled country houses, once the seats of cheerfulness and plenty, and the temples of the Most High ruinous and desolate, 'frowning in portentous silence upon the land.' The very mansions of the dead have not escaped violation Shattered fragments of armorial bearings, and epitaphs on scattered stone, attest the piety and vanity of the past, and the brutality of the present age.'"

APPENDIX.

APPENDIX.

(A.) Edmund Randolph was born in the city of Williamsburg, the capital of the colony of Virginia, on the tenth day of August, 1753. His father was John Randolph, Attorney General of the Colony, the son of Sir John Randolph, who had filled the same office, and been knighted for services performed in it to the Crown.

His mother was Arianna Jennings, the daughter of Edmund Jennings, Attorney General for the colony of Maryland.

Educated at William and Mary College, he early determined and prepared to follow the profession of his immediate ancestors, paternal and maternal, whose fame he afterwards worthily emulated and sustained. But his career was temporarily interrupted by the exciting occurrences of 1775, when ardently enlisting in the cause of the "rebellious" colonies against the oppressions of the Crown of England, he was disinherited by his father, who remained "loyal" to the Crown, and who sailed to England with Lord Dunmore, the Colonial Governor of Virginia.

Upon the appointment of General Washington to the command of the army of the confederated colonies, then investing Boston, Edmund Randolph became a member of his staff and secretary, and remained in that position during most of the siege. But having been adopted meanwhile as heir by his uncle, Peyton Randolph, the President of the first colonial Congress, who owned several large plantations in Virginia, and whose public duties precluded his attention to them, and who died in October, 1775, these occurrences compelled his return to Virginia and to civil life, to manage these estates, and the numerous slaves domesticated on them, with which he combined the active pursuit of his legal profession, early attaining in it high rank among the most prominent lawyers of his State. In the management of the large estates devised to him by his uncle, and of the numerous slaves upon them, he had no corresponding success His genial benevolence towards his slaves, and unwillingness to sell them, made his indulgence, to them proverbial among his acquaintances, and, as he afterwards admitted, "nearly ruined him" pecuniarily

On the 29th of August, 1776, he married Elizabeth Nicholas, daughter of Robert Carter Nicholas, Colonial Treasurer and Speaker of the House of Burgesses of Virginia.

In the same year, the people of Williamsburg elected him to the State Convention that framed the Bill of Rights, and the *first* and *best* written Constitution ever adopted, and before the close of the year they made him also their Mayor.— The Convention itself conferred upon him the office of Attorney General under the new Constitution, and at a subsequent session of the General Assembly, he was appointed its Clerk, an office of far inferior dignity *now*, than when it was filled by such men as Chancellor Wythe, and afterwards by William Wirt.

"His success at the bar was extraordinary. Clients filled his office, and beset him on the way from the office to the Courthouse, with their papers in one hand and guineas in the other. In 1779 he was deputed to the Continental Congress, and remained a member of it until 1782. In 1786 he was elected Governor of Virginia by the General Assembly, and was chosen by the same body one of the seven delegates to the Convention at Annapolis, and in the following year to the General Convention which had been summoned to revise the Articles of Confederation. In 1788 he was returned by the county of Henrico to the Convention, which was called to decide upon the Federal Constitution. In 1790 he was appointed by Washington the first Attorney General under the new Federal system, as he had been the first Attorney General of Virginia, thus filling an office which had been hereditary for three generations in his family. On the 2d of January, 1794, he succeeded Mr Jefferson as Secretary of State: an office which he held until the 19th of August, 1795, when he withdrew to private life, and resumed the practice of the law His person, his mode of speaking, the caste of his eloquence, as these appeared in his latter years, are described by Wirt, and 'will live in the pages of the British Spy.

"The history of this extraordinary man is the history of Virginia for the most interesting quarter of a century in her annals; and this history, although it has not seen the light, has been recorded by his pen. Mr. Wirt saw and consulted it while he was writing the biography of Patrick Henry. It is much to be regretted that it was destroyed by fire in New Orleans some years ago, while in the possession of his grandson of the same name, who then resided in that city, but has since died in California, and whose purpose it was to complete it. Of all the spheres of action in which Edmund Randolph moved, that in the Federal Convention held in Philadelphia in 1787 will especially attract the attention of posterity. His career in that body was surpassingly brilliant and effective, and, although he ultimately voted against the adoption by that body of the Constitution, because of what he deemed radical defects in it, which he had not succeeded in excluding, that instrument may be said perhaps to bear more distinctly the impress of his hand than that of any other individual. Nor was his course in the Virginia Convention of Ratification, (in which, for reasons there given, he sustained the Constitution,) less imposing."*

The debates of that Convention every where fully attest the learning, sagacity and eloquence which he there displayed.

The withdrawal of Edmund Randolph from the Cabinet of Gen. Washington in 1795 was made the occasion, and the causes of it, the subject of misrepresentations and calumnies by his political enemies, which, although at the time refuted and silenced by his "Vindication," then published by him, have been more recently revived and repeated in numerous publications in New England and New York, compiled or prepared from the private journals and correspondence of those same political enemies, by their descendants and others. Some notice therefore in this connection of these resuscitated partisan slanders is deemed due alike to the truth of history.

* Virginia Convention of 1776, by Hugh Blair Grigsby, Esq.

and to the memory of one of the purest and most illustrious men of Virginia.

The treaty with England, negotiated by Mr. Jay in 1794, had been received by the President and Cabinet in March, 1795—and at a called session, early in June, of the Senate, had been submitted for its advice upon the question of ratification. The character of the provisions of that treaty having become known in some measure to the people of the United States, had given rise to the utmost excitement and anxiety respecting them. By those who belonged to what was then called the Republican or Democratic party, it was considered that this treaty made to England concessions of the political, international and commercial rights of the United States, which were alike uncalled for, unjustifiable and humiliating to the national dignity and honor. Such were the views of it entertained by a portion of the Senate and by at least two of Gen Washington's Cabinet, Mr. Jefferson and Mr. Randolph. The Senate, by a barely constitutional majority, advised the ratification of the Treaty only *conditionally*, upon the consent of England to an omission of some of its obnoxious provisions. And a revival, at this time, of oppressive commercial restrictions by Great Britain made this more necessary. And in those views so fully did Gen Washington concur at that time, and until the withdrawal of Mr. Randolph from his Cabinet, that he repeatedly and persistently expressed his determination not to execute the treaty, except upon the express condition that these obnoxious provisions should be materially modified and amended by the British government, nor until these restrictions on American commerce were repealed by it.

Upon the resignation by Mr Jefferson of the position of Secretary of State, Mr. Randolph, who succeeded him, was left alone in the Cabinet to maintain these views of this treaty, and General Washington's position respecting them, against the vehement, urgent and persistent advocacy of the treaty by all the other members of the Cabinet To weaken or destroy his influence with General Washington, by exciting in the President's mind a suspicion of the sincerity and purity of Mr. Randolph's motives for his strenuous opposition to this treaty, became, therefore, an object of prime importance to its partisan advocates. Unfortunately an opportunity for doing this was accidentally afforded to them.

During the pendency of this question in the Cabinet, and indeed from the date of Mr. Jay's mission to England the Envoy to the United States of the French Republic, M. Fauchet, had manifested the utmost jealousy and ill-temper towards the Government of the United States because of what he deemed the great partiality of a majority of the Cabinet for England and English interests, and of what he did not hesitate to characterize as their ingratitude and treachery to France, evinced in their readiness and eagerness to make a treaty violative of existing treaties with France, and giving to England and English subjects rights and privileges which were withheld from the Republic and citizens of France.

To such an extent did he manifest this feeling, that he removed his residence from Philadelphia, and secluded himself in sullen displeasure at some distance in the country. This conduct on the part of the French minister, who had even suggested the possibility of a war with France, in the event of a ratification of Jay's treaty, excited in the mind of Gen. Washington much anxiety and concern; and he requested Mr. Randolph, the Secretary of State, to seek Mr. Fauchet in his seclusion, and to soothe and conciliate his irritated feelings, and his jealousy of what he called, with some reason, the confidential influence of the British Minister, Mr. Hammond, with some members of the Cabinet, by conferring with Fauchet, in a tone and manner, to some extent, frank and confidential. It will be seen that *it was the faithful execution of this wish of the President* which was perverted into the cause of all the calumnies against Mr. Randolph, and of his separation from the President, whose devoted and intimate friend he had been for more than twenty years.

These conferences between Mr. Randolph and M. Fauchet were by the latter made the subject of special dispatches to his government, in which, through misconception, exaggeration and inordinate vanity, in magnifying his own importance and that of his official services, he gave such versions of Mr. Randolph's communications to him as bore little resemblance to the originals, and were susceptible of the wildest misconception. A portion of these dispatches were captured at sea by a British frigate, and transmitted to Mr. Hammond, the British Minister at Philadelphia, who was just then, in conjunction with a majority of the Cabinet, most urgently pressing the ratification of Jay's treaty, and endeavoring to break down the opposition of what they termed the Democratic or French party, of which Mr. Randolph was the head.

The captured dispatches, without others therein referred to, and previously sent, but which were never recovered, left the meaning, even of their author, ambiguous if not unintelligible, but *by themselves* were capable of a construction, which seemed to impute to Mr. Randolph the extreme folly, if not criminal treachery, of having made to the French minister confidential communications violative of his official duty, and prompted by corrupt motives preposterously inadequate to tempt a man of even weak principle in his position—a construction afterwards emphatically disclaimed and denied by M. Fauchet himself. And among these communications imputed in this dispatch to Mr. Randolph were expressions disparaging and disrespectful to General Washington, which, if believed authentic, might well excite the indignation of the President as evidences of the basest treachery from one, who had so long been deemed by him his confidential and devoted friend.

Such an opportunity for destroying Mr. Randolph's influence with the President and of so securing the ratification of the British treaty, was eagerly and promptly seized upon by the British Minister and his coadjutors in the Cabinet

General Washington, then absent at Mount Vernon, was secretly written to, urging his immediate return to Philadelphia where these dispatches were secretly laid before him, and repeatedly deliberated on by him and those other members of the Cabinet in Mr Randolph's absence : until accidentally intruding upon one of these meetings of the rest of the Cabinet, to which, to his surprise, he had not been summoned, this garbled and exaggerated dispatch of the French Minister, which he had never before seen or heard of, was put into his hands, and an explanation of it required of him

Calmly and without any discomposure disclaiming all knowledge of the subject, but indignant at the treatment he had received, he instantly tendered his resignation of a seat in the Cabinet, and promised, as soon as practicable, to examine the paper then put in his hands, and make to it a written reply

That reply he accordingly soon made in the form of a pamphlet, addressed to the President, entitled "A Vindication of Edmund Randolph," which published by him in 1795, at *that* time refuted and silenced in the estimation of every candid and unprejudiced mind every suspicion, however slight, of his official fidelity and integrity, or personal honor, which Fauchet's garbled dispatches could have possibly aroused. That such was the judgment of his cotemporaries is shown by their correspondence at that time—among which may be cited a letter from Gen Gates to J. Wormley, Esq, dated New York, 11th January, 1796, and one from Mr Jefferson to Gov W. B. Giles, dated Monticello, 31st December, 1795, and more recently in the thoroughly partisan publication of J T Sullivan, entitled "Public Men of the Revolution," in which the author although giving the same version and interpretation to Fauchet's letter that has been adopted by all Mr. Randolph's political enemies, says: "At this day candor compels us to say that Mr. Randolph had no treasonable views with regard to his country.

In 1855 Mr. Randolph's "Vindication" having nearly passed out of print, and the calumnies which it had once silenced, having been revived by the numerous posthumous publications in New England, before referred to, a limited new edition of the pamphlet, with a Preface, noticing and replying to some of those slanderous publications, was published by one of his grandsons.

What is and will be the dispassionate judgment of posterity as to these calumnies, and the refutation of them is best expressed in a note to that admirable, accurate and philosophical work, published in 1857, "The Diplomatic History of the Administrations of Washington and Adams," by William Henry Trescott, Esq., and dedicated to the Hon. Edward Everett, with whom the author had been associated in the Legation to the Court of St. James. He says, p. 158. "The circumstances of Mr Randolph's resignation belong rather to the personal and party history of the day than to its diplomatic history For although they tended directly to increase the bias of General Washington's prejudice in favor of one section of his Cabinet, I do not think they seriously affected the course of events. To review them in detail would require a special chapter on the personal history of the times, a subject to me alike unpleasant and unprofitable

"The misconstruction of Mr. Randolph's conduct which in the then distempered state of public opinion was both natural and unfair, has not received historical sanction. The facts may be briefly stated thus: A dispatch from Mr Fauchet, the French Minister at Philadelphia, was intercepted by a British vessel, sent by the British Government to their Minister, Mr Hammond, and by him transmitted to the President, through the Secretary of the Treasury. This dispatch purported to be a full report of several conversations between Mr Randolph and the French Minister in which, according to the latter, Mr Randolph had given him a very distressing account of the factions in the country, and the divisions in the Cabinet; entered into a minute and indiscreet detail of the President's private views; and suggested to the French Minister certain ways of meeting a local combination against the Government in some of the States, which he construed into an implication of the venality of certain public characters These conversations were vaguely reported, and accompanied by a running commentary of insolent and inflated sentiment that makes it almost impossible to say what is fact and what fancy. This document was exhibited to General Washington just at the time when he was most troubled and annoyed by the opposition to Mr. Jay's treaty—that treaty being then under his consideration for ratification He submitted the dispatch to Mr. Randolph in a personal interview, and demanded an explanation in a manner that Mr Randolph considered evidence of a foregone conclusion, and of confidence already forfeited. He accordingly resigned, and addressed his vindication to the public In reference to the facts, I would only observe that no mere statement of the French Minister in the United States, during the period of their revolution, has any value as evidence. For without deliberately intending to misrepre-

APPENDIX. 59

sent, they took such strange and extravagant views of men
and things, and misunderstood so completely the relation of
measures and parties, that their opinions cannot be trusted;
and the whole of this very dispatch is conceived in that spirit
of ingenious, clever but extravagant misconception which is
the characteristic of the French revolutionary diplomacy—a
spirit which insisted upon treating the wildest political dreams
as the realities of political life. It is impossible to separate
what the French Minister calls Mr Randolph's 'precious
confessions'* from his own general narrative of American

---

*It is evident that the French word here used in M. Fauchet's dispatch,
'*precieux,*' was, whether through imperfect knowledge of the language,
or design, *mistranslated* for the President by Mr Pickering—Mr Randolph's
political enemy and successor in office. It was *then* used in *that translation*, as it has been in all the subsequent uncandid and slanderous publications already alluded to, in the *ironical, sarcastic* and *slang* sense, in
which the English word is sometimes used in conversation, implying *tur-
pitude, worthlessness* or *insignificance* a sense which every French scholar
knows the original did not admit of. Besides which, M. Fauchet, in his
subsequent certificate exculpating Mr Randolph, himself gives more ex-
plicitly his meaning in using this word showing that he used it in its seri-
ous, legitimate sense, as equivalent to "valuable," "important" and, if
unavailing, "costly" He says "On my arrival on this continent the President gave me the most positive assurance that he was the friend of the
French cause. Mr. Randolph often repeated to me the same assurance
It was impossible for me not to give faith to it, (in spite of some public
events relative to France which gave me some inquietude,) especially
when the Secretary of State constantly took pains, to convince me of the
sentiments of good will of his Government for my Republic. It was doubtless
to confirm me in this opinion that he communicated to me, without authority,
as I supposed, that part of Mr. Jay's instructions which forbade him to do
anything which should derogate from the engagements of the United States
with France. My error, which was dear to me, was prolonged only by the
continual efforts of Mr Randolph to calm my fears, both upon the treaty
with England and upon the effect which it might produce on France. He
was therefore, far from confiding to me any act any intention of government by virtue of any concert with me, or in consequence of any emolu-
ment received by him, or for the expectation or hope of any recompense
promised, or with any other view than to maintain a good harmony between
France and the United States. As to the communications, which he has
made to me at different times, they were only of opinions, the greater part,
if not the whole of which, I have heard circulated as opinions. I also re-
collect that on one occasion, at least, which turned upon public measures,
he observed to me that he could not enter into details upon some of them,
because by doing so he should violate the duties of his office, from whence
I have concluded and believe that he never communicated to me what his
duty would reprove. I will observe here, that none of his conversations

politics; and the absurd inconsistency of this fancy sketch of our politics is manifest to every student of our earlier history. But the charge of corruption, I cannot believe, was ever really believed, even by those small partisans who mistake malignity for honesty. Mr. Randolph belonged to a class of men who had faults and grave ones; they were passionate and prejudiced, but not treacherous; they were reckless and extravagant but not corrupt; and whatever were their failings, it might be said of that great old Virginia stock, as Fuller said of Woolsey, "truly nothing mean could enter into this man's mind." As to the indiscretion of such conferences with Fauchet, especially after the experience of French Ministers, which the government had suffered, that will depend upon the view taken of Mr Randolph's position of the Cabinet, and the political sympathies of the student. He endeavored to hold middle ground between the two sections, and in consequence, and I think unavoidably, was sacrificed. I would not have said this much, were it not that Mr. Gibbs in his memoirs of the Administrations of Washington and Adams, a work to which I have specially referred elsewhere, has devoted many pages of malicious ingenuity to the examination of Mr Ran-

with me concluded without his giving me the idea that the President was a man of integrity and a sincere friend to France. This explains, in part what I meant by the terms 'his precious confessions.' I proceed to other details relative thereto. I could allude only to explanations on his part upon matters which had caused to me some inquietude, and I have never insinuated, nor could I insinuate in that letter, that I suspected on his part even the most distant corruption. These explanations had equally for their object my different conversations upon western affairs, as may be seen in the sequel of this declaration.

"When I speak in this same paragraph in these words 'besides the precious confessions of Mr Randolph alone cast upon all which happens a satisfactory light.' I have still in view only the explanations, of which I have spoken above and I must confess, that very often I have taken for confessions what he might have to communicate to me by virtue of a secret authority. And many things, which in the first instance I had considered as confessions, were the subject of public conversations. I will say more—I will say that I have more than suspicions—that certain confidences which have been made to me were only to sound my private opinions, and the intentions of the French Republic, and I must appeal to the testimony of him who this day claims mine. He must know if I ever endeavored to meddle in the interior affairs of America, or even to influence, by any means whatsoever, the sentiments of men whose talents had called them to the head of affairs.

dolph's conduct, and concludes his review with these sentences. 'Mr. Randolph, in his vindication, gave many reasons against the probability of his guilt. There was produced soon after his resignation, one in favor of the supposition The investigation of his accounts conferred upon him the distinguished honor of being the first Cabinet officer who was a defaulter.' Vol. 1, p. 280.

"The facts are these, as proved by the official records in the proper Departments: Immediately upon his resignation, he surrendered the key of his public office to the door-keeper, and refused to cross its threshold again, thus leaving all his official papers to the custody of his successor, Mr. Pickering. An account of his administration was ordered and reported, 'covering the receipt and disbursement of over $1,000.000, which, according to the custom then, but no longer existing, passed through his hands on account of the maintenance of foreign diplomatic agents and intercourse. This account brought him in debt to the government On his part he immediately stated his account, making the government in debt to him, asserting his perfect confidence in the correctness of his account, and sustaining it by vouchers, so far as they were in his possession, and calling for the production of other vouchers, which he positively alleged were deposited by him in his own and other public offices, and remained in the custody of other public officers, but some of which were never obtained A suit was instituted by government to recover of him the balance reported against him, but upon several trials, the juries were divided, and no verdict could be obtained Mr. Randolph then proposed to leave the decision to the Solicitor of the Treasury—a proposition which clearly vindicated his confidence in his own integrity. That officer confirmed the *precise balance* reported against Mr. Randolph by the government account, and according to his agreement, judgment was entered up against him for that amount. To satisfy this judgment Mr. Randolph devoted every cent he possessed by conveying it to a trustee for that purpose, and it appears from the records of the Treasury Department that not only the entire balance, principal and interest, was discharged, but that, in consequence of the government having become the purchaser of a portion of the property conveyed in the deed of trust for its benefit, it had actually received, by a re-sale of that property, some seven thousand dollars more than the balance it claimed from Mr. Randolph. In addition to this the official records of this transaction show that, while every cent received by Mr. Randolph was charged to him with interest, no credit was allowed him, which was not supported by the voucher of the receipt of the agent of the government, to whose use it was *ultimately* applied: and that, where bills of exchange had been bought by Mr. Randolph, as Secretary of State, of merchants or bankers in this country, drawn on foreign merchants or bankers resident in the country to which the remittance to our foreign agent had been sent, the receipt of the person of whom the bill was bought was not allowed as a voucher, but that of the government agent abroad was required as indispensable, so that, if by any casualty resulting from the dangers of the sea, the existence of a general state of war in Europe, or the bankruptcy of foreign merchants or bankers, the foreign agent of our government failed to receive the remittance purchased for him here, *the Secretary of State had to bear the loss* and instances of this to large amounts are disclosed on the face of the accounts reported against Mr. Randolph, and acknowledged in the documents accompanying them In one of these cases the usual channel of remittance abroad, through Amsterdam, was cut off by the blockade of the coast of Holland; and it becoming necessary to remit to our Minister at Madrid, through bills on Madrid bankers purchased here, the bankruptcy of the parties to the bill occurring after the purchase of the bill, devolved upon Mr. Randolph a heavy loss under the rule mentioned. Add to this the principle universally adopted in government accounts of charging interest on all sums *received from* and allowing *no* interest on sums *due from* government: and it will be readily seen how easy it is to make out an account against a public officer, receiving and disbursing over one million of dollars, and that at a time when the administrative details of all the executive departments were more or less imperfect.

"In concluding this note, I ought to say that I was not able to conduct the above interesting and, I think, conclusive investigation directly I am indebted for it to one whose interest in Mr Randolph's fair fame guarantees the thoroughness, and whose character assures the conscientious accuracy of its detail. To say that I am responsible for the accuracy of its statements may be proper, but it can add nothing to its authority.

After Mr Randolph's return to private life he resumed and continued the practice of his profession in Richmond, until some three years before his death, when grief for the loss of his idolized wife, the affliction of seeing his talented accomplished and only son (for some years a distinguished lawyer even in his youth, and Reporter of the Court of Appeals of Virginia.) stricken down by paralysis, and premonitory attacks of the same disease so impaired his health and spirits that he may be said to have only lingered reluctant through his remaining years, until released by death on the 13th of September, 1813, in the county of Frederick, now Clark, at "Carter Hall," the residence of his relative, Col. Nathaniel Burwell, and was buried in the family cemetery of the Nelson family, familiarly known as the "Old Chapel graveyard." No good portrait of him, or of any of his immediate ancestors or descendants is now known to be extant, except one of his only son, Peyton Randolph, which is now in the possession of the widow of his grandson, Edmund Randolph, in San Francisco, California. There are in the possession of two of his granddaughters in Virginia, portraits of him and of his uncle, Peyton Randolph Sr., taken, it is believed, by Peale, but they were never considered likenesses by those familiar with the original and are therefore but little valued by their lineal descendants. A very beautiful full-length portrait of Peyton Randolph Sr., represented in full masonic costume, (by whom painted is unknown to the writer) was some years since destroyed by fire in the Library of Congress in Washington

---

* None of the Masonic records of Virginia extant give an account of Peyton Randolph's connection with the order, but in the proceedings of the Grand Lodge of the State, we find that in the session of A L 5784, (A D 1784.) Richmond Lodge, No. 10 was represented by Edmund Randolph, that in the session held Nov. 4th, of the same year, James Mercer was elected Grand Master, and he appointed Edmund Randolph Deputy Grand Master and in

Two beautiful miniatures of Sir John Randolph, and of his wife Susan Beverly, painted in England about the year 1740, are also in the possession of the family of Mrs. Wm. F. Wickham, (who was a lineal descendant from them,) in Hanover county, Virginia. Copies of these are in the possession of others of their descendants. Edmund Randolph, the last male descendant of this branch of the Randolph family of Virginia, a man of brilliant mind and of lofty character and accomplishments, died at the begining of a successful career in the profession of the law, in San Francisco, in the year 1861.

B. The following extracts from an article which was published in the London 'Herald and Genealogist' for August, 1866, will show that the generally accepted history of the family of the Father of his Country is based upon a very unsubstantial foundation:

THE WASHINGTON FAMILY.

'In the year 1791 Sir Isaac Heard, then Garter King of Arms, compiled a pedigree of the family of George Washington, then the first President of the United States, and transmitted a copy thereof to him, asking his opinion as to its correctness, and requesting him to add to it any other particulars within his knowledge. To this communication Washington responded on the 2d of May, 1792, thanking Sir Isaac

---

the session of October A. L. 5786, (A. D. 1786,) Edmund Randolph was unanimously elected Grand Master of Virginia, and he appointed John Marshall his Deputy. At the next annual convocation of the Grand Lodge, upon the petition of David Lambert, William Waddill and John Dixon, a charter was granted to Lodge No 19, named in compliment to the subject of this notice Richmond Randolph. It may not be inappropriate to add that both of the Lodges named in this note Nos. 10 and 19, not only still exist, but give promise of lengthy and useful careers.

The volume from which this information has been obtained, is in manuscript, and is the only record of the history of A. F. A. Masonry in this State, from 1777 to 1791. It has never been printed or copied, and with its loss would perish all our knowledge of the connection of the Randolphs, Blairs, Madisons, and other prominent men of the State and the nation, with the order. It is very properly in the charge and possession of that worthy and venerable brother, Dr. John Dove, for so many years the efficient Grand Secretary of the Grand Lodge of Virginia and to whom I am indebted for its examination.—ED.

for his attention, and sending certain information respecting the more modern history of his family, but confessed that it was a subject to which he had paid but very little attention and that he could not fill up with much accuracy the sketch sent him. This document, which was of considerable length, would now be almost priceless as an autograph, but it has unfortunately disappeared. A volume containing the original letter and other collections relating to the same subject passed subsequently, after Sir Isaac's death, into the possession of the late Mr. Pulman, Clarencieux. It was seen and examined by Mr. Jared Sparks when collecting materials for his biography of Washington, but cannot now be found.

Sir Isaac took as the basis of his pedigree the Heraldic Visitations of Northamptonshire in which the Washington family was included. Starting with the well-known fact that the first emigrants of the name to Virginia were two brothers named John and Lawrence Washington, who left England for that colony about the year 1657, he found recorded in the Visitation of 1618 the names of John and Lawrence described as sons of Lawrence Washington of Sulgrave in that county who had died in the year 1616. The names being identical with those of the Virginia emigrants, and the period at which they lived not altogether inappropriate, Sir Isaac *assumed* their personal identity, and on this assumption constructed his pedigree, deducing the descent of the American President through this heraldic family of Northamptonshire from the still more ancient one of the name in Lancashire. It is but just to the memory of Sir Isaac to say that he himself only regarded the pedigree as a conjectural one, and that he took the precaution to leave on the margin of his own copy a note (which was seen and copied by Mr. Sparks) to the effect that he was not clearly satisfied that the connection of the President with the Sulgrave family was or could be substantiated.

' Some years afterwards when Mr. Baker was preparing his History of Northamptonshire he pursued, in reference to his account of the Washington family, a precisely similar course. Either he acted independently, basing his pedigree on the same assumption, or, which is most probable, he had access to the collections of Sir Isaac Heard, and, presuming that Sir Isaac had thoroughly investigated the subject, adopted the pedigree which he had constructed. Sir Isaac's explanatory note, if seen, was ignored, and Baker confidently published the pedigree with the statements that John Washington of the Sulgrave family was afterwards of South Cave, in the county of York, that his brother Lawrence was a student at Oxford in 1622; that both emigrated to America about the year 1657, and that the former was the direct ancestor of the American President.

"This pedigree has ever since been received as authoritative by all the historians and biographers, everybody supposing that both Baker and Sir Isaac Heard had established the connection and descents by unimpeachable evidence, and no one dreaming for a moment of questioning the accuracy of their statements.

"The object of this paper is to prove that the conclusions of those eminent men, natural and reasonable as they may have been (which is not denied,) were nevertheless altogether wrong—in other words that the John and Lawrence Washington named in the Visitation of 1618 as the sons of Lawrence Washington of Sulgrave were not the emigrants to Virginia in 1657 and consequently that the former was not the ancestor of the illustrious President

"The first doubt cast upon Sir Isaac Heard's pedigree was perhaps unconsciously, by President Washington himself, and it is not unreasonable to suppose that it may have induced the former to record the note already mentioned. The language used by Washington in one portion of the letter referred to is important and suggestive. He says: 'I have often heard others of the family, older than myself, say that our ancestor who first settled in this country came from some one of the *northern* counties of England; but whether from Lancashire, Yorkshire or one *still more northerly*, I do not precisely remember.' Washington himself, when he wrote this, was about sixty years of age, and the memory of those older than himself, from whom he received the statement, must have reached back probably within half a century of the arrival of his first ancestor in Virginia. Traditions are valuable, or otherwise, as they are transmitted through the medium of ignorance or intelligence. In such a family as that of the Washingtons the original facts would be less likely to become perverted than if they had been successively communicated through persons of a less intelligent character. Taking the tradition, however, for what it may be worth, it is quite certain that Northamptonshire cannot be accounted 'one of the northern counties of England.' But Washington himself was perfectly clear upon this point, and, if his language means anything, it surely means that the county from which his first American ancestor emigrated, if not Lancashire, or Yorkshire, was one, as he says, 'still more northerly.' It must also be noted that he does not mention this locality as the ancient or original seat of the family, but says distinctly that his 'ancestor who first settled' in Virginia emigrated from that county.'

Then follows an analysis of the pedigree, as made out by Sir Isaac Heard and the evidence bearing thereon showing the errors into which he and Baker, the historian of Northamptonshire, had fallen, embracing too much matter in its details for our limited space, and continues:

"Referring again to the facts that the John and Lawrence Washington of the Northamptonshire pedigree were respectively at least sixty-two and fifty-five years of age in 1657, the date of the emigration, and that both of the real emigrants remarried and had issue in Virginia—facts, almost if not quite, sufficient in themselves to settle the question without further dispute, especially as the evidences in the will of Lawrence of Virginia indicate that he was probably under thirty years of age at the time of his emigration—we may safely leave the issue to the effect of either of the following propositions,—

"First. John Washington of Sulgrave and Brington was knighted, and became Sir John, while his brother Lawrence was a clergyman of the Established Church. If they were the Virginia emigrants the one must have abandoned his knighthood, and the other rejected his surplice and bands for both were never known in Virginia except as 'Esquires,' or

Gentlemen, and by the latter appellation they described themselves in their wills. For either of these rejections there could have been no possible cause, as Virginia was then a loyal colony, and her established religion that of the mother country.

Secondly. Sir John Washington had at least two wives. The first, named Mary, was buried as Islip, in Northamptonshire, while the name of his widow was Dorothy, and she was buried at Fordham in Cambridgeshire. John Washington gentleman, the Virginia emigrant, states distinctly in his will dated the 27th of September, 1675, that he brought his first wife from England with him, that she died in Virginia, and was buried with two children on his own plantation, and that his second wife's name was Anne, whom he appointed his executrix.

"It is clear, therefore, that if John Washington son of Lawrence and Margaret of Sulgrave, was identical with Sir John Washington of Thrapston, knight, he could not have been the emigrant to Virginia in 1657; and, as there cannot be the slightest doubt upon that point, the assumption of Sir Isaac Heard and Mr. Baker unquestionably falls to the ground."

C. Robert Rose Rector of Albemarle Parish, who died in Richmond, Virginia in July, 1751, and whose grave is marked by a handsome monument in the burial ground surrounding St. John's church in that city, was a very prominent man in the colony. He left a diary which he had carefully kept during the last six years of his life, in which nearly every family in Virginia, of any standing at the time he wrote, is mentioned. A transcript of it is in the possession of the editor, and with the assistance of gentlemen well informed on all matters relating to the persons and subjects mentioned in it, he has been engaged in preparing it for the press. If published, it promises (in the opinion of those best qualified to judge) to be one of the most interesting books relating to the colonial history of Virginia ever published. In the notes to it will be found an almost complete *Vade Mecum* of the genealogy of Virginia families—and among these a lengthy notice of the family of Beverley. An account of Mr. Rose will be found in Bishop Meade's "Old Churches and Families of Virginia."

BOOK PLATE OF
Robert Bolling of Chellowe,
Author of the Memoir.

ROBERT BOLLING,
The Husband of Jane Rolf,
(The grand-daughter of POCAHONTAS.)

JOHN BOLLING,

(The Son of Jane Rolf.)

MARY KENNON,
The Wife of John Bolling.

Boston Public Library.
JOHN BOLLING, JR.

ELIZABETH BLAIR,
The Wife of John Bolling, Jr.

THE BOLLING ARMS.
(See page. 42.)

RICHARD RANDOLPH,
Of Curles.

JANE BOLLING,
The Wife of Richard Randolph,
Of Curles.

RICHARD RANDOLPH, Jr.,
Of Curles.

ANNE MEADE,
The Wife of Richard Randolph, Jr.

THOMAS BOLLING,

Of Cobbs.

BETTY GAY,
The Wife of Thomas Bolling of Cobbs.

JOHN BLAIR,
Of the Supreme Court of the United States,
a miniature in the possession of Hugh Blair Grigsby, Esq

The Rev. Hugh Blair.

WM. BOLLING,
Of Bolling Hall.

MARY RANDOLPH,
(Wife of Wm. Bolling,)
Daughter of Richard Randolph of Curles.

ANN MEADE BOLLING,
Daughter of Col. Wm. Bolling.

CPSIA information can be obtained
at www.ICGtesting.com
Printed in the USA
LVHW081910060323
741056LV00004B/57